RISE ABOVE SERIES
2

I0233056

SPIRITUAL DIMENSION
PROTOCOL

For Victorious Life

IN THE

Spiritual Dimension

Reed D. Tibbetts

SPIRITUAL DIMENSION PROTOCOL
© 2017 by Reed D. Tibbetts

Published by Insight International, Inc.
contact@freshword.com
www.freshword.com
918-493-1718

All Scripture quotations, unless otherwise noted, are taken from the *New American Standard Bible®*, © 1960, 1962, 1963, 1968, 1971, 1972, 1973, 1975, 1977, 1995 by The Lockman Foundation. Used by permission.www.Lockman.org

Scripture quotations marked "KJV" are taken from the King James Version of the Bible.

ISBN: 978-1-943361-22-9
E-book ISBN: 978-1-943361-23-6

Library of Congress Control Number: 2016958587

Printed in the United States of America.

ENDORSEMENTS FOR
SPIRITUAL DIMENSION PROTOCOL

"I have known my friend, Reed Tibbetts, for thirty-six years. I am convinced that Reed is a man of absolute integrity. He is a diligent student of the Bible. He is comfortable in his relationship with the Holy Spirit. I am anticipating further Biblical teachings from Reed Tibbetts."

— Richard C. Benjamin Sr.,
Apostle and Founding Pastor of
Abbott Loop Christian Center,
Anchorage, Alaska

"Reed serves faithfully and loyally as one of the elders in the church I pastor. He is one of the best theological minds I have had the privilege of calling my friend. His teachings are a unique mix of potent ingredients that form a special recipe of the truth, and reach the minds and spirits of those he teaches. Relax, receive, and enjoy the concepts of his latest book."

— Mike Connaway, Senior Pastor of
VLife Church, McKinney, Texas
and Author of *My Third House*

"Reed Tibbetts is one of the most preeminent theologians I have ever met. He brings his steeped knowledge of the Bible, and uses his God-given anointing, to write books that encourage and challenge all believers to grow in their relationship with God. Reed has a great ability to reach all generations in his writings and teachings. He is truly a man of God."

— Gabriel Kvalvik, faithful member of
the *I Serve* team at VLife Church,
McKinney, Texas

DEDICATION

I dedicate this book, "<u>Spiritual Dimension Protocol</u>" to my wife Janis. We have been married for over forty-six years, and she has been a unique strength for me, decade after decade. Over the last eleven years the Lord has taken me for quite a trip in learning about how to sense, understand and walk in the spiritual dimension, and she has been my fellow traveler, though it has been difficult. It has not been a smooth path, for there are times that I am not a fast learner; some might say I am thick-headed. Through every stumble, every mistake, every attack of the enemy, every time I retreated in fear, every time the truth became clear, Jan has been there, helping me rejoice in the truth, or get back in touch with the Holy Spirit and His truth. Back in 2005 when I struggled through "the transparent wall," and my misinterpretation landed me in a place of deep fear, she was there to speak God's truth and to pray me through. When, at times I have practiced battling Satan and demons in a zealous, but inaccurate way, she has faithfully supported me and walked with me. When I have made a major breakthrough in understanding the truth about how to walk in the spiritual dimension, and I have shared the truth with her, often pontificating and going on and on and on, she has patiently listened and helped me fine tune it. And when I have put the subject in writing, she has read it, carefully editing and suggesting clarity. Interestingly enough she has accomplished all of this, while at the same time being my primary care provider (I am a disabled vet). I have many friends and family that love me dearly, and I appreciate them so much. But Jan is the one who loves me the most and helps me the most. I love you, sweetheart!

CONTENTS

WHY THE RISE ABOVE SERIES?

Isaiah 2:2, 3 – The word which Isaiah the son of Amoz saw concerning Judah and Jerusalem. Now it will come about that in the last days the mountain of the house of the LORD will be established as the chief of the mountains, and will be raised above the hills; and all the nations will stream to it. And many peoples will come and say, "Come let us go up to the mountain of the LORD, to the house of the God of Jacob; that He may teach us concerning His ways and that we may walk in His paths." For the law will go forth from Zion and the word of the LORD from Jerusalem.

Micah 1:1; 4:1, 2 – The word of the LORD which came to Micah of Moresheth…And it will come about in the last days that the mountain of the house of the LORD will be established as the chief of the mountains. It will be raised above the hills, and the peoples will stream to it. Many nations will come and say, "Come and let us go up to the mountain of the LORD and to the house of the God of Jacob, that He may teach us about His ways and that we may walk in His paths." For from Zion will go forth the law, even the word of the LORD from Jerusalem.

Matthew 5:14-16 – You are the light of the world. A city set on a hill cannot be hidden; nor does anyone light a lamp and put it under a basket, but on the lampstand, and it gives light to all who are in the house. Let your light shine before men in such a way that they may see your good works, and glorify your Father who is in heaven.

Matthew 28:19, 20 – Go therefore and make disciples of all the nations, baptizing them in the name of the Father and the Son and the Holy Spirit, teaching them to observe all that I commanded you; and lo, I am with you always, even to the end of the age.

John 10:10 – The thief comes only to steal and kill and destroy; I came that they may have life, and have it abundantly.

All of these Scriptures are talking about the church of the Lord Jesus Christ in the last days, describing how people from all nations and people groups will come into the church. It is all about the end times ingathering of people into the kingdom of God and the church of our Lord.

Back in the eighth century B.C., during the reigns of the Kings Ahaz and Hezekiah in the nation of Judah, we had two very different scenarios of what happened to the house of God (the Jerusalem temple). It can be summed up very simply: King Ahaz closed the doors of the house of the LORD (II Chronicles 28:24); King Hezekiah opened the doors of the house of the LORD (II Chronicles 29:3). There were also two prophets (Isaiah and Micah) who spoke identical prophecies about the very last days. Isaiah came from an aristocratic family, while Micah was a peasant farmer: two very different classes, but an identical prophecy from the LORD. This end time prophecy, through shadow and substance, tells the end times church exactly how people will be attracted to and come into the church of the Lord Jesus Christ.

The mountain of the house of the LORD, the mountain of the LORD, the house of the God of Jacob, Zion and Jerusalem are all terms referring to the temple in Jerusalem, where God's presence resided. In the New Testament, the church is the temple of God, for His presence resides inside every person who has accepted Jesus Christ as Savior and Lord. This is what the Old Testament prophecy is saying to the church:

- In the last days the church of the Lord Jesus Christ will be raised above all other religions, philosophies and movements. As it is established as chief among all religions, many people from all nations and all kinds of people groups will come into the church, looking to learn the ways of the LORD and how to walk in His paths. Simply put, there will be a large group of people who will become Christians.

This is what I referred to earlier as the end times ingathering. We want this to happen, and it is clearly the will of God, for He is not willing for any to perish, but for all to come to repentance (II Peter 3:9). So how will the church rise above the hills, that is, the religions, philosophies and movements of the world? The answer is found in the teachings of Jesus during the Sermon on the Mount. The church becomes like a city set on a hill: it can't be hidden. The people in the church will be a light that shines out to all people. We are to shine in such a way that they see our good works and glorify God. Our good works are our very lives: our abundant lives. People will see the abundant lives that we live in Jesus, and come into the church to learn more; they will marvel at the ways of the LORD that give us abundant life, and accepting Christ, they will walk in the same abundant lives that we show them.

We have used many methods to shine forth our light and spread the gospel (T.V., internet, social media, evangelism crusades, door-to-door witnessing, street preaching, picketing, political involvement, etc.) and we spend millions of dollars on those methods. But are we seeing the end times ingathering, with masses of people coming into the church? Certainly not in the United States. So I ask another question: are we living the abundant life in Jesus Christ that shows itself as far superior to other religions, philosophies and life styles? Are the people of the world looking at the people in the church and saying, "Wow! Their lives are far superior to and way above anything we are seeing or experiencing. Let's go into the church of Jesus Christ and check it out!" The answer is no. On a one-to-one scale, there are some individuals who come into the church for this very reason, but not on the massive scale spoken of in the prophecies of Isaiah and Micah.

We, the church of Jesus Christ, need to focus our attention on living the successful, powerful, abundant life that God has for us. In every aspect of life: marriage, child-raising, work, business, finances, physical health, mental health, spiritual dimension, etc., we need to live our lives in such a way that it shines brightly and brings people into the church to check it out. Instead of settling for a so-so or struggling life, and making it to heaven by the skin of our teeth; or being content that we are moral and live stable prosperous lives, we need to live the abundant life that results in many coming into the church. So the books of the "Rise Above" series are all about Christians learning to walk in the abundant life. Rise above, and see the harvest of people coming into the church to learn the ways of the Lord and how to walk in them. Many people will come to Jesus Christ to have the abundant life!

Spiritual Dimension Protocol is a book about functioning in the spiritual dimension in the authority and power that every Christian should have in their abundant life. Enjoy it, learn and increase your abundant life. Rise above!

INTRODUCTION

I tried to come up with catchy words and a catchy title that would pique your curiosity, so that you would jump in and read this book. I thought about that colorful character, "Q," from the TV series, "Star Trek: The Next Generation." He was from the "Q Continuum," but I couldn't make that work for my title. Whether I called it "The H Continuum," for heavenlies, or "The S Continuum," for spiritual, it really wasn't a continuum that I was addressing. I realized that the underlying premise for the book was to contrast the place where we function primarily through our physical bodies, with the place where we function primarily through our spirits. I tried "realm," and "kingdom," but the word that seemed to fit the concept best was "dimension." Throughout the book I use the phrase spiritual dimension for the place we are to function through our spirits. I really wanted to help each of us to sense, understand and walk in the spiritual dimension. We need to know the proper way to function in the spiritual dimension, and in His Word, God has given us the clear plan and instructions for how to do that. It is God's protocol for the spiritual dimension, and we must be willing to see it, embrace it and use it.

Dictionary definitions of protocol carry a lot of different nuances of meaning, but I am using the term in the sense of the original, best and correct plan of conduct that God has laid out in His Word, for functioning in the spiritual dimension.

My pastor often speaks a message of encouragement that counteracts doubt and fear. He usually says something like this: "How many of you believe that God exists? How many of you believe that the Holy Spirit is inside of you? How many of you believe that there is a heaven and a hell? How many of you believe that there is a real devil? How many of you believe that you are saved and will be going to heaven when you die? Are you sure?" To each of these questions he always gets a strong response in the affirmative. Then he says something like this: "So you believe in an invisible God that you have never seen, and you believe that a ghost, the Holy Ghost, is inside of you, and you believe in a wonderful place we will go to after we die, even though you haven't seen it, and you believe in a devil you have never seen?" People respond with a strong yes. "Then you are full of faith, because it takes a lot of faith to believe in all that. Don't worry about doubt or fear: you are full of incredible faith!" All of us need to live as the "full of faith" people that God has made us.

My desire in writing this book is to help every one of us, as Christians, to sense, understand and walk in the spiritual dimension, just as God intended. We are spiritual beings with bodies, and that means God designed us to function in both the physical dimension and the spiritual dimension, or as Paul calls it in the book of Ephesians, in the "heavenlies." Now stop and think about that for a minute. God created humans to be multi-dimension dwellers. The angels (including the fallen ones) were not created to dwell in both the spiritual dimension and physical dimension. Of course God dwells in every dimension all the time. But only humans are uniquely created to dwell in both dimensions at the same time. Now it doesn't take a brain surgeon to see that most humans function well in the physical dimension, but few function, even a little, in the spiritual dimension. Satan has used fear and lies to keep us intimidated and reticent to walk in the spiritual dimension; but God wants us to tap into His truth and our inner faith and carry out our assignment, as His spiritual warriors. To carry on my silly Star Trek metaphor: we need to boldly go where few Christians have gone before. My personal goal is to function as well in the "heavenlies," as I do on the earth. And I believe you want that also. Read on, brothers and sisters, and allow God's spiritual protocol to set you free to walk in victory in the kingdom of heaven, by faith!

You must be a true, born again Christian to walk in faith, without fear, in the spiritual dimension. Going to church does not make us Christians. Hanging around Christians does not make us Christians. Performing religious acts does not make us Christians. Only by accepting the free gift of eternal life from Jesus and inviting Him to come into our hearts and lives can we be saved and begin our life of faith, victory and power in the spiritual dimension.

If you have done this, you have the necessary presence and power of God within you for your spiritual dimension existence. If you have not, I invite you now to become a Christian. Pray this prayer right now, and you will be born again and begin establishing your powerful position in God.

"Dear Jesus, thank you for dying on the Cross for me. Please forgive my sins and come into my heart and life. I step down from the throne of my heart, and ask you to sit there. I will fear no evil, for You are within me. Help me connect with Your power and presence, so that I can live the abundant life you want me to live. I accept that I am saved by faith and grace. I love you Lord. Amen."

Chapter One

THE TRANSPARENT WALL

The surgery lasted over 9 hours. Lumbar vertebrae fusion was completed; titanium rods, brackets and screws were in place; punctures around the spinal cord were sealed, and I lay in the recovery room.

For over a year I had been battling lower back and leg pain. They called it degenerative disc disease; I just wanted to get rid of the pain! I self-medicated with heavy doses of over the counter pain killer, and then prescription pain pills. Using a walker to get around, I had become a chair potato. Things came to a crisis point one Sunday morning, when I awoke to severe back pain that would not quit, no matter how I moved. The ambulance ride to the emergency room and the transfer to a hospital bed resulted in screaming pain… my screaming. Once they got me on to IV morphine medication, I drifted off into sleep. Over the next two weeks multiple tests, steroid shots, myelograms, and a laminectomy with disc trimming; and still the severe pain persisted. So the decision was made to perform the major surgery.

Pain medication and anesthesia do something to your consciousness. Those two weeks in the hospital before the surgery, I was on constant IV morphine, and everything around me in the physical world seemed surreal. After the lengthy surgery, I was in the recovery room for two hours, and they had some difficulty getting me to come out from under the anesthetic. The good news is that the constant severe pain was finally gone, and I could begin the long recovery. Over the next few days, I had several visitors (friends and family) come to my hospital room, with words of encouragement and prayer. My wife was almost constantly by my side. I appreciated all the time and conversation with people during this time. But something was happening.

They were malevolent, with hate in their eyes, and they wanted to get to me to hurt me in some way.

As I was talking to my wife, I could see something behind her. It was a transparent wall, and on the other side of it I could see several beings; all trying to get through the wall. They were malevolent, with hate in their eyes, and they wanted to get to me to hurt me in some way. It filled me with fear, and I didn't know what to do. I blinked several times, hoping the whole thing would disappear, but it didn't. I re-focused on my wife and carried on the conversation with her, hoping again that they would disappear. But they didn't. And this wasn't just a one-time experience. It was almost constant over several days. It was the most fearful time in my life. These beings I was seeing hated me and were out to kill me. They clawed at the wall; they rushed and bumped it; they tried reaching around the wall at the sides. Hour after hour, day after day they were there. I realized that no one else could see them, and it was as though I was aware of two realities at the same time. At times I could get really involved in the conversation with people who visited me, and the transparent wall and beings would not bother me so much, but it was all still there.

The only time it seemed I could turn off my awareness of these beings and the transparent wall was when I would cry out to God and quote to myself the Scripture: "For God has not given us a spirit of fear, but of power and love and a sound mind." (II Timothy 1:7 KJV). I would tell myself that the stark fear I felt could not be from God, and I would exhort myself to use my sound mind to embrace the truth: the truth that the malevolent beings were not real; the transparent wall was not real and I had nothing to fear. "You shall know the truth and the truth shall make you free." (John 8:32). The fear was so strong that I would have to repeat the scripture and the thought process over and over, again and again; it became a lengthy mantra until finally my soul was quiet enough to allow me to fall off to sleep. God, in His mercy would finally grant me rest.

But what I thought was the truth was correct in the Scripture, but wrong in the circumstances. Over the next year, I was hypersensitive to spiritually evil things. I couldn't watch certain movies because they would touch upon the spiritual realm, evil spirits, demons, etc. And that would set off the fear in my inner being again. My wife and others often prayed for me, to help me overcome the fear. I believed all the beings and the transparent wall were not real, but just a hallucination. Never the less anything that would remind me of that "transparent wall" time in the hospital would bring strong fear to me again. It was no way to live, because the fear was a bondage that kept me from being all that God wanted me to be.

"Did the demons ever get
through the wall to touch you,
to harm you, to kill you?"

And then God set me free. He let me know that He has given to me a spirit of power and love and a sound mind. He confirmed that when I knew the truth, I would be free. He let me know that the transparent wall and the malevolent beings were real! He showed me that I am a spiritual being, and that I exist in the physical dimension and in the spiritual dimension. As a born again Christian, my spirit is born again, and the Holy Spirit of God dwells inside of me. I have physical senses through which I perceive the physical dimension, and I have spiritual senses by which I perceive the spiritual dimension. When I saw the malevolent beings in the hospital, I was seeing the spiritual dimension, and they were real: I was not hallucinating. When I saw the transparent wall in the hospital, I was seeing the spiritual dimension, and the wall was real: I was not hallucinating. What I was seeing was real, no matter how much I chanted that it was not real. Even though I was wrong in what I thought was the truth, God in His mercy would grant me rest and calm, so that the fear did not overwhelm me. Then He showed me the full truth. Yes, I am a spiritual being, and I exist in the spiritual dimension; and there are malevolent beings (the devil and the demons) in the spiritual dimension that hate me and want to destroy me. And yes there is a transparent wall. But it is not a wall of revealing by which I can see and fear the demons; it is a wall of protection by which God protects me! God asked me: "Did the demons ever get through the wall to touch you, to harm you, to kill you?" "They did not and cannot because I am with you and in you and protect you." (Greater is He who is in you than he who is in the world. I John 4:4). This revelation from God shocked me…illuminated me…and set me free!

Chapter Two

THE THIRD HEAVEN

II Corinthians 12:2-4 – I know a man in Christ who fourteen years ago – whether in the body I do not know, or out of the body I do not know, God knows – such a man was caught up to the third heaven. And I know how such a man – whether in the body or apart from the body, I do not know, God knows – was caught up into Paradise and heard inexpressible words, which a man is not permitted to speak.

There have been two theories put forth, attempting to explain the "third heaven" language. **The first idea** is that it refers to levels of spiritual heaven – In this idea the first heaven is the overall spiritual dimension that contains the good and the bad place; the angels and the demons. The second heaven is the part of the spiritual dimension where only the good forces can be; God and His angels. The third heaven is the inner good place, the throne room of God. **The second idea** is that it refers to physical and spiritual places. The first heaven is the atmosphere of the earth, the second heaven is outer space, where all the planets and stars are, and the third heaven is Paradise, where God is on His throne in the spiritual dimension. Most scholars believe that Paul here is referring to the second idea. It doesn't matter to my point, but I prefer to think it is the first idea, with Paul actually experiencing things in the throne room of God, just like John the Beloved experienced in the book of Revelation.

Now what is this about? Is Paul rhetorically speaking about himself, or did this event happen to another? Paul uses such stark and vivid language in presenting this happening that it lends itself to being interpreted as his very own experience. Paul cited this at the conclusion of listing his many experiences in the Lord, and seems to make it his own in verse seven, tying his own thorn in the flesh to the revelation. I do think it happened to Paul. And it was phenomenal! He states twice that he does not know if it was an in the body or out of the body experience. Was Paul taken bodily into God's heaven, or did his spirit leave his body behind as he was taken to the third heaven? But God definitely does know. God was so "in" this experience, that Paul rests assured that God knew exactly what happened. While in Paradise, Paul heard words that a man is not allowed to speak. We have no idea what the content was, but it enters the unique area of having been heard by a man, who then was not allowed to let us know the message. There are only two other places in Scripture where this happens.

Daniel 8:26 —The vision of the evenings and mornings which has been told to you is true; but keep the vision secret, for it pertains to many days in the future. Daniel had been given a vision that covered the coming Macedonian kingdom, the Ptolmaic Period, the Roman Empire, etc. Then it touched upon the first century and probably the end of time. Verse fourteen mentions an end time period of time; 2300 evenings and mornings. But he is told not to reveal that part of the vision. So we don't know what details that end time period of time refers to.

Revelation 10:4 — When the seven peals of thunder had spoken, I was about to write; and I heard a voice from heaven saying, "Seal up the things which the seven peals of thunder have spoken and do not write them. " John was given a revelation that had a lot of information about the future, and especially end-time events. Between the sixth and seventh trumpet, one-third of mankind had died, and there were seven peals of thunder. Whatever they spoke, we do not know because John was told not to write them down.

Paul says that because of the surpassing greatness of the revelation he was given, to keep him from exalting himself ("I am something special because God took me to heaven and let me hear these words!"), he was given a thorn in the flesh.

The third heaven experience shows us clearly that there is a spiritual dimension above and beyond the physical one.

Paul was caught up to the third heaven and couldn't tell whether it was an in the body or an out of body experience. Daniel was lying on his bed and saw a dream and visions in his mind. John was in the Spirit on the Lord's Day and heard and saw all of what is recorded in Revelation. A lot of people see all of these experiences as something that happens in our mind; whether we're in the Spirit, dreaming or having visions. Maybe it's real; maybe it's just "imagination." But you and I know when we are dreaming, and these Scriptural incidences were far more than that. I believe that Paul and Daniel and John were having real experiences in the spiritual dimension. The third heaven experience shows us clearly that there is a spiritual dimension above and beyond the physical one, and that a Christian can exist in both dimensions, and have important experiences in the spiritual one.

Chapter Three

STEPHEN SAW INTO THE SPIRITUAL DIMENSION

Acts 7:55,56 – But being full of the Holy Spirit, he gazed intently into heaven and saw the glory of God, and Jesus standing at the right hand of God; and he said, "Behold, I see the heavens opened up and the Son of Man standing at the right hand of God."

Stephen had been taken before the Council, formally accused of blaspheming God. He presented a lengthy defense of himself and the gospel of Jesus Christ. He called his accusers stiff-necked and uncircumcised in heart, and said they were always resisting the Holy Spirit. The Jews reacted in burning anger, and rushed to stone Stephen. As they were about to execute him, he suddenly saw into the spiritual dimension!

"I see the heavens." He saw the glory of God and Jesus standing at the right hand of God. Some have said that Stephen was blessed with this vision to set the joy of his future in heaven before him, as he was about to experience a grue-some death. But I believe he was seeing the present reality of his Savior in the spiritual dimension, not a future hope, but a present reality. By the Holy Spirit he exercised his spiritual senses and saw the glory of God.

The spiritual dimension is always there, but we cannot perceive it with our physical senses. How did it happen that he could suddenly gaze into the spiritual dimension? Taking a closer look, I see two important things.

(1). He was full of the Holy Spirit. Now every Christian believer has the Holy Spirit inside of them, and Scripture does indicate that we can experience a subsequent event, usually referred to as being baptized or filled with the Holy Spirit (Acts 2:4, 8:15-17, 10:44-46, 19:6). Stephen, along with most of the Christians of his time, had already experienced salvation and baptism with the Holy Spirit. But it seems that at certain times the Holy Spirit manifested Himself strongly in the individual believer, something that Scripture calls "being full of the Holy Spirit."

In Acts chapter four we see this expressed twice with Peter. On the day before, Peter and John had experienced a phenomenal day! By the power of Jesus Christ, Peter had healed the lame man at the Beautiful Gate, and then preached his second evangelistic sermon, resulting in 5,000 people accepting Christ. On that high note, Peter and John had been arrested and thrown into jail; the priests and the Sadducees were greatly disturbed that they were preaching and teaching about the resurrected Jesus. So the next day the rulers, elders and scribes, including the high priest and his "high priest" party, had Peter and John brought before them to answer for their actions. *Acts 4:9 – "Then Peter, filled with the Holy Spirit, said to them…"* At this critical point in time, Peter was wholly dependent upon and reaching for the Holy Spirit within him. And the Holy Spirit responded, filling Peter in a special way, in order to speak boldly. After Peter proclaimed Christ Jesus to them, the authorities threatened Peter and John and released them. Peter and John then went to their companions and related the whole story to them. The whole group prayed fervently together asking for God's help so that they could speak His word with all confidence. *Acts 4:31 – And when they had prayed, the place where they had gathered together was shaken, and **they were all filled with the Holy Spirit** and began to speak the word of God with boldness.* At this point in time, they were all wholly dependent upon and reaching for the Holy Spirit within each one of them. And the Holy Spirit responded, filling them in a special way, in order to speak boldly!

For Stephen, at this critical moment, he reached inward to grasp the power and presence of the Holy Spirit. The Holy Spirit responded, filling him in a special way, and he could see into the spiritual dimension!

So he focused on the Holy Spirit and the spiritual dimension with all his strength. And he suddenly saw Jesus!

---

(2). He gazed intently into heaven. We have quite a few examples of Christians putting intensity into their gaze. In Acts 3:4 Peter fixed his gaze upon the lame man as he was about to heal him in the name of Jesus. Acts 10:4 indicates that Cornelius, who was having a vision from the Lord, fixed his gaze on the angel in the vision. In Acts 11:6 Peter fixed his gaze upon the sheet in his vision. Acts 13:9 records Paul fixing his gaze on Elymas, just before he pronounced blindness on him as a judgment for his opposition to the gospel. In Acts 14:9 Paul fixed his gaze upon the lame man in Lystra, just before speaking his healing. We all understand, just as they did in the first century, that we need to be intense about the really significant, profound and deeply spiritual things. How often have we spoken to our children, as we correct them: "Look at me when I'm talking to you!"? If something is really important we need to focus our attention on it, to the exclusion of other things that might distract us. Here Stephen is not fixing his gaze or intensity on something in the physical dimension, or on a vision or dream. Instead, he zeroed in on the spiritual dimension. He was in front of the high council and the chief priest, and they were gnashing their teeth at him. He knew they were about to kill him. So he focused on the Holy Spirit and the spiritual dimension with all his strength. And he suddenly saw Jesus!

Acts 7:59, 60 – They went on stoning Stephen as he called on the Lord and said, "Lord Jesus, receive my spirit." Then falling on his knees, he cried out with a loud voice, "Lord, do not hold this sin against them!" Having said this, he fell asleep.

And so Stephen made the transition. He put off his physical body and transitioned into the spiritual dimension that he was seeing so clearly as he was facing imminent death.

Chapter Four

TRANSITIONS

Our primary focus needs to be on the best way for us, as physical beings, to sense, understand and walk in the spiritual dimension. But right now I would like to look at the transition that happens when we die. It should help us better understand the spiritual dimension. First let's look at some unusual transitions: when men made the transition without dying.

Enoch

Genesis 5:21-24 – Enoch lived sixty-five years, and became the father of Methusaleh. Then Enoch walked with God three hundred years after he became the father of Methusaleh, and he had other sons and daughters. So all the days of Enoch were three hundred and sixty-five years. Enoch walked with God; and he was not, for God took him.

Hebrews 11:5,6 – By faith Enoch was taken up so that he would not see death; and he was not found because God took him up; for he obtained the witness that before his being taken up he was pleasing to God. And without faith it is impossible to please Him, for he who comes to God must believe that He is and that He is a rewarder of those who seek Him.

Jude 1:14 – It was also about these men that Enoch, in the seventh generation from Adam, prophesied, saying, "Behold, the Lord came with many thousands of His holy ones, to execute judgment upon all, and to convict all the ungodly of all their ungodly deeds which they have done in an ungodly way, and of all the harsh things which ungodly sinners have spoken against Him."

When God gives you specific prophecy to speak, like He did with Enoch, it is an exercise of your spiritual senses to hear it.

Enoch's story is a tremendous illustration of relationship with and faith toward God. Enoch had a close relationship with God, described as walking with God. During his life we know that he prophesied of future events, when God would judge ungodly people. Prophecy is revelation from the Holy Spirit that addresses current events and/or predicts future events. In order to receive prophecy from God, a person needs to hear in the spiritual dimension. When God gives you specific prophecy to speak, like He did with Enoch, it is an exercise of your spiritual senses to hear it. Enoch was given the witness that his kind of "faith" walk with God was especially pleasing to Him. When God gives you a witness that your faith/conduct is pleasing to Him, you need to be close to Him in the spiritual dimension to hear it. I think that God enjoyed their close relationship so much that he simply took Enoch into the spiritual dimension full time! By faith it happened that way. So the usual transition of death did not happen for Enoch.

Elijah

II Kings 2:9-11 – When they had crossed over, Elijah said to Elisha, "Ask what I shall do for you before I am taken from you." And Elisha said, "Please, let a double portion of your spirit be upon me." He said, "You have asked a hard thing. Nevertheless, if you see me when I am taken from you, it shall be so for you; but if not, it shall not be so." As they were going along and talking, behold, there appeared a chariot of fire and horses of fire which separated the two of them. And Elijah went up by a whirlwind to heaven. Elisha saw it and cried out, "My father, my father, the chariots of Israel and its horsemen!" And he saw Elijah no more. Then he took hold of his own clothes and tore them in two pieces.

Luke 9:28-32 – Some eight days after these sayings, He took along Peter and John and James, and went up on the mountain to pray. And while He was praying, the appearance of His face became different, and His clothing became white and gleaming. And behold, two men were talking with Him; and they were Moses and Elijah, who appearing in glory, were speaking of His departure which He was about to accomplish at Jerusalem. Now Peter and his companions had been overcome with sleep; but when they were fully awake, they saw His glory and the two men standing with Him.

Elijah had ministered for many years as a prophet to the nations of Judah and Israel, at a time when many in the land followed after false gods, and did not honor Jehovah. He had performed many miracles that clearly showed God was the only true god, and that the followers of false gods would suffer. There were times that he felt like he was the only one left who served the living God. His devotion to God was complete, but he was not perfect. He had a nature just like you and me; sometimes weak, sometimes strong. The end of his ministry was near, and he had raised up a successor in Elisha. So the two of them went for a final stroll. Suddenly a chariot of fire and horses of fire appeared, and separated the two of them! Then a whirlwind grabbed Elijah and he was taken into heaven (the spiritual dimension). Here, just as it was for Enoch, the usual transition of death did not happen for Elijah. He was seen again, hundreds of years later, when Moses and Elijah appeared on the Mount of Transfiguration. Peter, John and James got to see into the spiritual dimension (described as appearing in glory, as His face and clothes became white and gleaming).

People tend to think that for their whole life on earth, the focus is on everything physical around them, in this world. Christians know that they have instructions for how to conduct themselves in the world, and how to conduct themselves in the spiritual dimension, but they tend to focus on the things of the earth, and the rules of earthly conduct, and leave the spiritual dimension things for the future. The way they see it, after they die, the focus will be on everything spiritual. While our conduct here on earth is important, the truth of Scripture is that our spiritual dimension conduct, while we are alive on earth, is the more important thing

Ephesians 6:12 – For our struggle is not against flesh and blood, but against the rulers, against the powers, against the world forces of this darkness, against the spiritual forces of wickedness in the heavenly places.

Ephesians 6:2 – Set your mind on the things above, not on the things that are on earth.

You could say that we have two lives or two phases to our life. Death is two things: **it is a transition and a transformation**. In our first life phase, we are born as physical/spiritual beings (physical body, soul and spirit) that start as primarily in the physical dimension, and then through spiritual rebirth in Christ learn to function in the spiritual dimension. The time comes that we make the transition to our second life phase, in which we are spiritual/physical beings (spiritual body, soul and spirit) who exist primarily in the spiritual dimension, and then as God plans and directs we will participate in the physical dimension. In order to transition to our second life phase, we need to be transformed by God. Our body (container) which has been totally physical, becomes spiritual (we are raised a spiritual body).

Chapter Five

I HEARD HIS SPIRIT LEAVE HIS BODY

**There was no mistake; when I heard Bill's yell,
I knew it was the sound of his spirit leaving his body.**

In 1970 I was an army combat medic, serving in Viet Nam. In May of that year President Nixon authorized troops to go into Cambodia, in order to destroy major parts of the "Ho Chi Minh Trail." This trail was used by the enemy to bring supplies out of North Viet Nam, through Cambodia and into South Viet Nam, to the Viet Cong and regular NVA soldiers that were there. I was part of the First Air Cavalry Division at the time. Back in the United States, the president was very unpopular with the Democrats, the press, and the anti-war movement because he expanded the conflict into another nation. But in our unit we were extremely glad he authorized the action. My platoon had been operating close to the Cambodian border, and on more than one occasion we were attacked by quickly moving units of NVA, that would then dash back across the border. We were not allowed to pursue them, or even to shoot across the border. It was extremely frustrating. After the President's authorization, we moved on in, and we had successfully routed NVA troops and captured an underground base, along with munitions, supplies and vehicles. After about three weeks we were flown by helicopter up to the highlands to continue the mission. We were moving at company strength (about 130 men). On our first day in the highlands one of the squads (eight men) from my platoon left the perimeter to set up a trail ambush site, while the rest of us broke for lunch. But the squad walked right into an NVA ambush. Someone was shot and the cry "Medic!" was immediately sounded. I took off running through the high grass to reach the wounded. When I got close I came under heavy enemy fire, and squad members were screaming at me to get down. I flattened and began to low crawl through the grass, but it was so thick and tall that I couldn't find the wounded man. In a low voice/whisper I said, "Joe....where are you?" Immediately an automatic burst from an AK47 was loosed by the enemy, and I was struck twice in my left leg. The burst had been fired at my voice...that's how close we all were in the ambush. Yet we couldn't see each other – friend or enemy – because of the tall thick grass. I ripped my pants open to see the damage, and had to tie a tourniquet on, in order to stop the bleeding. Then I proceeded to crawl around, eventually finding Joe. I tied bandages on two separate wounds; one minor, one very serious. As I was doing this the fire fight continued around me. At one point I heard Bill scream out. It was a piercing yell/shout/scream/wail; and I knew that he was dead. There was no mistake; when I heard Bill's yell, I knew it was the sound of his spirit leaving his body. I treated another wounded man, and then crawled over to Bill. He was quite dead, having taken a direct hit to the head. After more fire fight, we had a Cobra gunship fly over and make two passes with the mini-guns firing. The mechanical scream of those mini-guns is another sound I will never forget. That broke up the ambush, and we evacuated back to the perimeter. Along with Joe (who died in the chopper) and Bill (who was dead), I was flown out on a Medivac helicopter. I was taken to a field hospital (MASH) to be stabilized, then on to Saigon where I underwent major surgery. Two days later I was in Japan where I underwent another surgery, then back to the states. That was the end of my war time.

What remains a vivid memory to me, even after 44 years, is that I knew Bill was dead before I ever got near him. It was that final yell. I knew in the very core of my being that it was the sound of his spirit leaving his body. Maybe other people have experienced something similar. Someone might dismiss it as my "vivid imagination." But that's what happened. To put it into the language of my present understanding, when our physical body dies, our soul and spirit do not stay in the physical container. We do not stay asleep in our physical body until the resurrection of the dead. And we are not left as naked spirits. Instead we move on to our spiritual container.

I Corinthians 15:44 – It is sown a natural body, it is raised a spiritual body. If there is a natural body, there also is a spiritual body. So also it is written, "The first man, Adam, became a living soul." The last Adam became a life-giving spirit. However, the spiritual is not first, but the natural; then the spiritual. The first man is from the earth, earthy; the second man is from heaven. As is the earthy, so also are those who are earthy; and as is the heavenly, so also are those who are heavenly. Just as we have borne the image of the earthy, we will also bear the image of the heavenly.

Paul is talking about what happens to us when we die. Our spiritual body (spiritual container) is of a heavenly nature. In other words we no longer have the container that ties us so tightly to the physical dimension. We have a new container that is very "spiritual dimension" friendly!

But just because our present body ties us tightly to the physical dimension, it doesn't mean that we can't sense the spiritual dimension. On the day of Bill's death, I sensed a "spiritual dimension happening," when his spirit and soul left his physical body and moved on to his spiritual body. If I could sense the spiritual dimension back then, I should be able to train my spiritual senses to discern the spiritual dimension now. Then I heard his spirit leave his body. Now I should be able to sense what the Lord wants me to sense in the spiritual dimension.

Chapter Six

THE HEAVENLIES

Ephesians 1:3, 4 – Blessed be the God and Father of our Lord Jesus Christ, who has blessed us with every spiritual blessing in the heavenly places (the heavenlies) *in Christ, just as He chose us in Him before the foundation of the world, that we would be holy and blameless before Him.*

Ephesians 1:18-21 – I pray that the eyes of your heart may be enlightened, so that you will know what is the hope of His calling, what are the riches of the glory of His inheritance in the saints, and what is the surpassing greatness of His power toward us who believe. These are in accordance with the working of the strength of His might which He brought about in Christ, when He raised Him from the dead and seated Him at His right hand in the heavenly places (the heavenlies), *far above all rule and authority and power and dominion, and every name that is named, not only in this age but also in the one to come.*

Ephesians 2:4-7 – But God, being rich in mercy, because of His great love with which He loved us, even when we were dead in our transgressions, made us alive together with Christ (by grace you have been saved), and raised us up with Him, and seated us with Him in the heavenly places (the heavenlies) *in Christ Jesus, so that in the ages to come He might show the surpassing riches of His grace in kindness toward us in Christ Jesus.*

Ephesians 3:8-10 – To me, the very least of all the saints, this grace was given, to preach to the Gentiles the unfathomable riches of Christ, and to bring to light what is the administration of the mystery which for ages has been hidden in God who created all things; so that the manifold wisdom of God might now be made known through the church to the rulers and the authorities in the heavenly places (the heavenlies).

Ephesians 6:10-13 – Finally, be strong in the Lord and in the strength of His might. Put on the full armor of God, so that you will be able to stand firm against the schemes of the devil. For our struggle is not against flesh and blood, but against the rulers, against the powers, against the world forces of this darkness, against the spiritual forces of wickedness in the heavenly places (the heavenlies).

The heavenlies is referring to the several levels of the spiritual dimension.

In the New Testament heaven is referenced hundreds of times. The Greek word that I have translated as the heavenlies, is used eighteen times. Five times it refers to the place we go in the future when we die. Thirteen times it is referring to something that we experience now, while we are still physically alive on the earth. Incidentally Paul is the one who used the word seventeen times, and John used it once (in John 3:12 in the context of people being born again). The particular Greek word is "epouranios." It is a combination of the simple word used for heaven hundreds of times: "ouranos", with the addition of the prefix "epi." This prefix has the basic meaning of "upon" or "above." The word could mean: super heaven, or higher heaven. I have seen a number of scholars translate it as "the heavenlies," in Ephesians, and I will run with that. Looking at Paul's use of the word throughout Ephesians should help us understand and appreciate the concept. The heavenlies is referring to the several levels of the spiritual dimension.

God has a deep love for us; so much so that He sent His son Jesus to die on the cross for us, so that we have been reconciled to God and now have Him inside of us. Jesus came so that we might have abundant life, and the Father has blessed us with every spiritual blessing in the heavenlies. God wants us to experience our new abundant life, both on earth and in the spiritual dimension. Knowing that the spiritual dimension is a challenging and dangerous place, He has blessed us with every spiritual blessing in the spiritual dimension. "Every spiritual blessing" is a pretty broad statement, but it's meant to be. Whatever we need in the spiritual dimension for sustenance, for sensing, for functioning, God gives us. That should give us great confidence. We do not need to be fearful of the spiritual dimension; we are protected and equipped with every spiritual blessing He gives us!

God raised Christ from the dead and seated Him at His right hand in the heavenlies. Sometimes in our attempt to grasp the working of our triune God, we get notions that seem to separate the Godhead. We think the Father is in heaven, and that Jesus went away to be in heaven, seated at the right hand of the Father, and the Holy Spirit is left here with us, in the physical dimension. But that's not right. The fullness of the Godhead dwells in Jesus in bodily form (Colossians 2:9). That Galatians statement was made about twenty years **after** Jesus died, was resurrected and ascended to the Father. When I think about God being inside of me, I don't just think about the Holy Spirit. I think about Jesus; I think about the Father. I believe that all of God is within me. In the same way, we need to look at this concept of Jesus being seated at the right hand of the Father. As I have often heard said, there's not going to be three separate thrones in heaven – one for the Father, one for the Son, and one for the Holy Spirit. We need to realize that the concept of being seated at the right hand of an authority is referring to a position of favor and power, not a location. Jesus has the position of supreme authority in the spiritual dimension. It is a concept of ultimate power, strength and might. He is far above all rule and authority and power and dominion. Now here's the dynamite kicker: we are seated with Him at the right hand of the Father in the spiritual dimension. That means we have the position of power, strength and might, far above all rule and authority and power and dominion in the spiritual dimension! That is why we can sense, understand and walk in the spiritual dimension with confidence and without fear.

So as we are gaining confidence to walk in the spiritual dimension, what do we do there? These Scriptures show us a couple of things. God wants us to spread the gospel, so that more people come to repentance and experience the saving grace of God through Jesus Christ. When we are seeking His kingdom and His righteousness, we minister the love of Christ to others, and the will of the Lord is accomplished. Something else happens at the same time. We reveal and make known the manifold wisdom of God to the rulers and authorities in the spiritual dimension. The spiritual dimension has angels and archangels, and demons and whatever you call the head demons. Well, God has chosen that the rulers and authorities in the spiritual dimension – whether good or bad – learn of His manifold wisdom through the church; through us. As I spread the truth and gospel of the Lord to people in the world (the physical dimension), I also declare the manifold wisdom of God to the rulers and authorities in the spiritual dimension. That is positive spiritual dimension functioning and ministering. Now, as I try to do what God wants me to do in the world, there are times that people oppose what I am trying to do. Maybe that has happened to you at one time or another. There are organizations out there that oppose everything Christ wants us to do. But humans in the physical dimension are not the real enemy. We are involved in a battle and we had better fight against the true enemy. This Scripture says that we fight/struggle against wicked rulers and forces in the spiritual dimension. The Greek word literally means "wrestle." Now I really like this as I think about it. This is like a hand to hand combat that we can't lose! All the power, strength and might we need are available to us in the spiritual dimension; and get this – our fellow tag team member is the Lord Jesus Christ Himself. How can we lose?

The "heavenlies" are the spiritual dimension. We are spiritual dimension beings. As we learn more about our mission, our power, our authority and our protection, we can better sense, understand and walk in the spiritual dimension, as God wants us to.

Chapter Seven

ABOUT THAT MANSION IN HEAVEN

John 14:2, 3 – In my father's house are many mansions: if it were not so, I would have told you. I go to prepare a place for you. And if I go and prepare a place for you, I will come again, and receive you unto myself; that where I am, there you may be also. (KJV)

John 14:2, 3 – In My Father's house are many dwelling places; if it were not so, I would have told you; for I go to prepare a place for you. If I go and prepare a place for you, I will come again and receive you to Myself, that where I am, there you may be also.

The idea many people see here is that Jesus is in heaven preparing a place for us. When we die, or for those still living when the 2nd coming of Christ occurs, we will be taken to our special place in heaven (mansion). But could there be a more immediate "spiritual dimension" meaning?

I have never believed that some day in heaven I will sit on a cloud and play a harp. Nor do I believe that I will stand around marveling at streets of gold. I can't picture myself relaxing in a mansion, taking it easy in the presence of the Lord. My God is so much bigger and higher than that. I believe that everything God has us doing now on the earth and in the spiritual dimension is preparatory work and training to equip us for the task and mission we will be doing for the Lord in eternity. So I see a deeper meaning in these verses from John chapter fourteen.

I go to prepare a place for you...that where I am, there you may be also...Having completed the spiritual dimension task Jesus sat down at the right hand of the Father, in the heavenlies...and we are seated with Him at the right hand of the Father in the heavenlies!

That's where He is, and that's the place
He was preparing for His disciples,
so that they could function in that spiritual dimension.

The Father's house may refer to heaven. But in John 2:16 Jesus used the phrase in referring to the temple He had just cleansed of animals, coins, money changers and sacrifice sellers. "Stop making my Father's house a place of business." And Paul indicates the household of God is the church of the living God (I Timothy 3:15). It is possible Jesus was saying that in His church there are many places/positions that His people are to occupy. He was going to prepare and make ready the place for His people to occupy. The Greek word for place may also be translated space or region or realm. When He died and was resurrected, He fully achieved the plan of salvation for mankind. Consequently He has the position of ultimate power and authority in the spiritual dimension, and His people also have this position of power and authority because of what He did. He defeated death, hell and the grave and has been given the position of authority and power far above all rule and authority and power and dominion in the spiritual dimension. And that is our position too! Jesus fully functions in the spiritual dimension because He died and was resurrected. That's where He is, and that's the place He was preparing for His disciples, so that they could function in that spiritual dimension.

Jesus was preparing His disciples for the coming events. He wanted them to know that He was accomplishing something for them, and He would be back. They probably didn't understand any of what He was saying. But some sixty years later, John the Beloved, recorded what Jesus said because he did see and understand what Jesus meant. Along with the first century church, he had experienced the reality of sensing, understanding and walking in the spiritual dimension. Jesus left His disciples to go to the Cross. When He was resurrected He came again to them. He had prepared the place for them! Along with Him they were conquerors and spiritual dimension dwellers.

It is true that our future with the Lord in the new heavens and earth is going to be glorious. But it is also true that we are to be successful spiritual dimension dwellers with Him, here and now. Before any Christian could be a powerful warrior in the spiritual dimension, Jesus had to die on the cross and rise again from the dead. By doing that He became the ultimate authority in the heavenlies, and He then shared that position of ultimate power and authority with us! He prepared the place for us to successfully occupy: spiritual dimension victory. That is far more important than some mansion we may be thinking about for the future. With authority and power we stride forth as the people and army of God, to success and victory in both the physical dimension and the spiritual dimension!

Chapter Eight

GOD'S KINGDOM - WHICH DIMENSION?

There is a lot said about God's kingdom in the Scripture. The phrase "kingdom of God" is used 68 times in 10 different New Testament books. The phrase "kingdom of heaven" is used 32 times, only in the book of Matthew. "Kingdom of God" and "kingdom of heaven" are almost always synonymous. Most of the time the kingdom referred to is not a physical kingdom, but something in the spiritual dimension; something that exists within our being, because we are in the Holy Spirit and the Holy Spirit is in us. With our souls and spirits we sense, understand and walk in the kingdom of God. The benefits of our spiritual dimension activity in the kingdom can be felt and experienced in the physical dimension (such as physical healing), but the eternal effects are spiritual dimension benefits.

The Jewish people of the first century were fixated on the kingdom of God being an earthly kingdom. Whether it was the scribes and Pharisees, or His very own disciples, they were very fixed on the coming Messiah establishing His kingdom here on earth. They believed the Romans would be defeated and Israel would be established again as His kingdom on earth. The Pharisees did not believe that Jesus was the Promised One; His disciples did believe that He was the Messiah: the Christ, the son of the living God! But was Jesus looking to establish His kingdom in this world?

Luke 17:20,21 – Now having been questioned by the Pharisees as to when the kingdom of God was coming, He answered them and said, "The kingdom of God is not coming with signs to be observed; nor will they say, 'Look, here it is!' or, 'There it is!' For behold, the kingdom of God is in your midst (literally "within you").

Jesus wanted inquiring people, especially his disciples, to see that there was a much bigger picture, beyond the limits of this physical dimension. His kingdom was not to be found on the physical earth; but within His people; a concept distinctly of their souls and spirits. But, as I said, they were really fixated on the earthly kingdom coming.

Acts 1:6-8 – So when they had come together, they were asking Him, saying, "Lord, is it at this time You are restoring the kingdom to Israel?" He said to them, "It is not for you to know times or epochs which the Father has fixed by His own authority; but you will receive power when the Holy Spirit has come upon you; and you shall be My witnesses both in Jerusalem, and in all Judea and Samaria, and even to the remotest parts of the earth."

Even after Jesus had been crucified, buried and rose again from the dead; even after He had appeared to them many times and told them to wait in Jerusalem and they would be baptized with the Holy Spirit in just a few days; even after all that, they were still focusing on the establishing of a kingdom here on earth, in the physical dimension.

Luke 23:42 – And he was saying, "Jesus, remember me when you come in Your kingdom. And He said to him, "Truly I say to you, today you shall be with Me in paradise."

Here we have the thief and the Lord relating to the kingdom as the place that Jesus would rule after their deaths. The thief knew they were both to die, since they were being executed by crucifixion. He was asking Jesus to remember him in His kingdom. Jesus understood exactly what the thief meant, and He responded that the thief would be with Him, that very day, after they had died, in Paradise. Paradise was understood to be the good place in the spiritual dimension, where people went after they died. Jesus equated Paradise with His kingdom.

John 18:36 – Jesus answered, "My kingdom is not of this world. If My kingdom were of this world, then My servants would be fighting so that I would not be handed over to the Jews; but as it is, My kingdom is not of this realm."

John 3:3 – Jesus answered and said to him, "Truly, truly, I say to you, unless one is born again, he cannot see the kingdom of God."

But when we are born again of the Spirit, our spirits are untwisted and enabled.

Jesus Christ did not see the earth (the physical dimension) as His kingdom. His kingdom was in the spiritual dimension! We are created with a physical body, a soul and a spirit. Our physical body makes it easy for us to sense, understand and walk in the physical dimension. Because of sin, our spirit becomes twisted and disabled, so we cannot properly sense, understand and walk in the spiritual dimension. But when we are born again of the Spirit, our spirits are untwisted and enabled, and we can see, to live and move and have our being in His kingdom…in the spiritual dimension. His Holy Spirit lives inside of us to help us function as spiritual beings. He wants us to function fully in the spiritual dimension.

Since we have physical bodies, and it is easy for us to live and move and have our being in the physical dimension, we tend to focus on the physical, and leave the spiritual for the future…someday, when Jesus returns, or when we die, then we will focus on the spiritual dimension. But is that what God wants?

God's kingdom is not about eating and drinking (physical dimension), but instead it is all about the Holy Spirit leading us in righteousness, peace and joy (spiritual dimension) (Romans 14:17). Jesus Himself told us not to worry about food, clothing and shelter (physical dimension), but instead to seek first His kingdom and righteousness (spiritual dimension) (Matthew 6:25-33).

Colossians 3:1 – Therefore if you have been raised up with Christ, keep seeking the things above, where Christ is, seated at the right hand of God. Set your mind on the things above, not on the things that are on earth.

We know that Christ is seated at the right hand of the Father in the heavenlies (the spiritual dimension). We are commanded to keep seeking the things there; to set our minds on the things there, in the spiritual dimension. For us, now, in the present church age, God's kingdom is in the spiritual dimension, and we must do all we can to sense, understand and walk there.

Chapter Nine

TIMOTHY LEARY

Ten years ago I had a traumatic year physically. It culminated in my hospitalization for several weeks. During that time I was on morphine for pain, almost all the time. I also had two minor surgeries and two major operations, with the liberal use of anesthesia. Needless to say, I was drugged more in those few weeks than I had been in all my previous life. I had bizarre hallucinations and some very troubling spiritual dimension experiences. Some people dismissed it all as unreal hallucinations, but I came to realize that some of it was real, and that the drugs had impacted my spiritual dimension senses. It made me think a lot about what drugs might be doing to many people in our society. Certainly food for serious thought.

LSD was discovered by Albert Hofmann in 1938. At that time the drug was not noted as having any beneficial effect, so its study was discontinued. Five years later in 1943, Hofmann took up his experiments again. While creating the synthetic form, he accidentally ingested a small amount, and experienced 2 hours of "not unpleasant" mild hallucinations, seeing fantastic pictures, and extraordinary shapes with an intense kaleidoscopic play of colors. More experimentation followed. LSD was introduced to the public in 1948, and hailed as a cure-all for a number of ills, including psychiatric disorders and alcoholism. Thousands of studies involving the drug proliferated starting in the late 1940's and going all the way into the early 1970's. Over 40,000 patients were treated with it. Dr. Timothy Leary, a psychology professor at Harvard University, used the drug extensively and experimented at length with it. He popularized the drug and is known for the LSD catch phrase: "tune in, turn on and drop out." By the early 1960's, backlash had built up against Dr. Leary and his co-professors, and He was fired from Harvard. The drug status was changed to an illegal controlled substance by the mid 1960's. But by that time the counterculture had been "turned on," and did not give up the substance that had been life-altering for them. Mass use of LSD during the hippie years is said to have collectively changed the culture, as thousands experienced spiritually changing effects from the drug

Using drugs does something to impair and
suppress our physical dimension senses,
and to tweak our spiritual dimension senses.

Controlled experiments and uncontrolled use and abuse of all kinds of "mind expanding" drugs multiplied. Use of drugs affects the sense receptors in the brain. I would put it this way: using drugs does something to impair and suppress our physical dimension senses (sight, hearing, smell, touch and taste), and to tweak our spiritual dimension senses. People who use drugs understand their effect upon the physical senses, but are usually not aware that the spiritual senses are also being affected. Drug experiences can open the soul to interaction in the spiritual dimension, and to the influence of seducing and deceiving spirits. It is not accidental that the Haight-Ashbury District in San Francisco, which was like the Central Station of the drug-use movement in the 60's, now has witches, warlocks and sorcerers, practicing astrology and spiritism.

Some of the people who have gone on these drug-induced trips report reaching a state of fear: being gripped with a sense of fear, and being desperately frightened. Some experience a sense of being detached completely from their physical body, and then seeing with their spirit eyes: cathedrals, hallways, tunnels, corridors and other worlds. They say they saw things that they had never seen before on the physical and spiritual planes; things that have always been there, but they couldn't see them previously. I cite all this to point out that humans, apart from the Lord Jesus Christ, still experience the spiritual dimension. Many who want to sense the spiritual dimension use drugs to enhance this goal. But they don't know how dangerous that is!

Please understand me: I do **not** advocate the taking of any mind-altering drugs. But it is a mistake to dismiss all the things people on drugs have seen or experienced as mere hallucinations. Some of the things people experience while on drugs, or under anesthesia are not real. But some are real in the spiritual dimension, and should not be lightly dismissed.

When a person is born it is an act of procreation. A man, a woman and God act together to create a human with physical body, soul and spirit. As a person grows and commits sin *(for all have sinned and fall short of the glory of God – Romans 3:23)*, it has an impact on his whole being; body, soul and spirit. His spirit is twisted and disabled. Consequently he cannot sense, understand or walk in the spiritual dimension as God intended. But he does still have a spirit, and he can experience the spiritual dimension. Satan and his demons can fight, damage and win against him. He can be defeated and even possessed by demons. And make no mistake; Satan wants to destroy him. But if that person accepts Jesus Christ as his Savior and Lord, God comes to live inside of him and his spirit is born again: untwisted and enabled to function in the spiritual dimension as God intended. Having God inside of him makes all the difference *(because greater is He who is in you than he who is in the world – I John 4:4)*. With Jesus Christ inside of him, and having the same position of power and authority in the spiritual dimension as the Lord has, he has the upper hand and can defeat Satan and his demons in any battle.

Chapter Ten

THE KEYS TO THE SPIRITUAL DIMENSION

Matthew 16:18, 19 – I also say to you that you are Peter, and upon this rock I will build my church; and the gates of Hades will not overpower it. I will give you the keys of the kingdom of heaven, and whatever you bind on earth shall have been bound in heaven, and whatever you loose on earth shall have been loosed in heaven.

Christ had asked his disciples: "Who do you say that I am?" Peter had responded: "You are the Christ, the Son of the living God." Jesus responded very positively to Peter's statement, declaring that it had been revealed to him by His heavenly Father. Then He declared that He would build His church upon Peter's confession. He further said the He would give Peter the keys to the kingdom of heaven, and things would be bound and loosed on earth and in heaven!

Matthew 18:17, 18 – If he refuses to listen to them, tell it to the church; and if he refuses to listen even to the church, let him be to you as a Gentile and a tax collector. Truly I say to you, whatever you bind on earth shall have been bound in heaven; and whatever you loose on earth shall have been loosed in heaven.

In this passage Christ was delineating a process for how a Christian should interact with a fellow Christian who sins. If the sinning Christian will not listen, the next to last step is to tell the whole situation to the church, in hopes that he will repent and be won. If he fails to listen and change, he is to be regarded as a Gentile and tax gatherer. Then Jesus indicates the same concept He communicated to Peter. He said the church would have the power and authority to bind and loose on earth and in heaven.

We (the church) have the keys to the kingdom...the keys to the spiritual dimension. With those keys whatever we bind or loose on earth (the physical dimension) shall have been bound or loosed in heaven (the spiritual dimension).

> **The keys given were at the least a clear expression of control and power, and possibly an expression of ownership.**

Keys of the kingdom of heaven. When you buy a new home, it usually takes awhile for all the paperwork to be completed. But at the closing everything is finalized, and you are given the keys to the house. It is now yours: you own it! When you are a jailor, you have many prisoners locked in their cells. You have the keys to the jail, and that means that the prisoners stay in their cells, or get set free by your action. You have the control, the power over what happens to the prisoners in the jail. When a policeman takes a suspect into custody, he puts handcuffs onto the suspect, in order to exercise physical control over him, while he is transporting him to a location in which he can be secured with greater control. He has keys to the handcuffs, so he can release the suspect, when appropriate. He has authority and control over the suspect. When someone famous or popular is honored by a city, they are usually given the key to the city. It is a symbolic gesture expressing appreciation and honor, but it doesn't give the person of honor any real power, authority or ownership. All that being said, in this context Jesus was not just speaking a symbolic action. Because He then expresses the concept of loosing or binding, the keys given were at the least a clear expression of control and power, and possibly an expression of ownership. The keys were given to Peter in the context of (1) properly identifying Jesus Christ and (2) Jesus building His church. The same loosing and binding power and authority were spoken of with regard to the church. So the church (including its leaders) has been given the keys to the kingdom: used in the physical dimension and the spiritual dimension. A case has been made that the authority and power of the keys is not for all Christians, but just for church leaders. After considering the context of Matthew 16 and Matthew 18, I have to conclude that the use of the keys is not limited to church leaders, but is available to everyone in the church who names Jesus Christ as their Savior and Lord. The key thing to remember is that these are the keys to the kingdom of heaven (spiritual dimension}.

Binding and Loosing. The terms for binding and loosing can be applied broadly. The Greek word for bind (deo) can mean to bind, to tie, to lock away or prevent. The Greek word for loose (luo) can mean to loose, to untie, to release or set free. These words can be applied to tying up bundles of hay for storage, and then breaking them apart to feed the cattle. They can also be used with regard to "do's" and "don'ts" of doctrinal practice. They were used in applying or lifting a curse; also magical formulas to get good things or bad things. They were also used about prisoners being locked away or set free. These terms were also used of the person who is demon-possessed (bound); when the demon is cast out, he is loosed. Christians, functioning within the church, and with the Holy Spirit inside of them, are to bind what needs to be bound, and loose what needs to be loosed.

Sequence and tenses. The tenses, voices and moods of the verbs, participles and conjunctions used in these two passages are complicated, and can be misunderstood. I am not going to go into the nitty-gritty details, but rest assured that I did a careful analysis to get the correct meaning. I will say that the tenses, voices and moods of the verbs and participles in these two passages are exactly parallel and exactly the same. So the meaning of binding and loosing from Matthew chapter sixteen is exactly the same as the meaning in Matthew chapter eighteen. The best expression of the meaning is this: If and when you bind or loose a thing on earth at a specific point in time, then that thing will be bound or loosed as a completed action with continuing results in heaven. **When at a point in time you bound or loosed a thing in the physical dimension, then that thing will have been bound as a completed action that has ongoing or continuing results, in the spiritual dimension.**

Whatever. Whatever you bind…and…whatever you loose. In our current society the word "whatever" seems to mean something so vague and huge that it is unimportant, or to be disregarded. It carries a flavor of disrespect: you know, when a teen girl says to her dad, "Whatever." Or it may mean something is indefinite. But in this Scripture it is quite important, very definite and something to be regarded seriously. As I have read many commentaries on these passages of Scripture, I have found many attempts to limit the application of the use of the keys and the binding and loosing of things. They attempt to look at the immediate and greater context to conclude that it must refer only to doctrine, or to excommunication in the church. Not one of these interpretations addresses the use of the word "whatever." Two words, a relative pronoun and a conjunction combine together to be translated "whatever." Within those two words are some flavors of meaning: "as great or as much," "whatever is expected to occur." It is pretty wide open, and "whatever" is the best word to use. So whatever we bind or loose in the physical dimension, within our expectations and within the will of the Lord, will be bound or loosed in the spiritual dimension. "Whatever" is wide open and very inclusive.

We have the keys to the kingdom of heaven! In the coming chapters we will learn more about how we bind and loose things in the physical dimension, so that they are bound and loosed in the spiritual dimension. The biggest and best way to bind and loose is to learn the truth, speak the truth and do the truth. Every deception can be neutralized by the appropriate truth. Every truth is a key. **We (the church) have the keys to the spiritual dimension. We should use them!**

Chapter Eleven

OPEN HIS EYES LORD

II Kings 6:15-20 – Now when the attendant of the man of God had risen early and gone out, behold, an army with horses and chariots was circling the city. And his servant said to him, "Alas, my master! What shall we do?" So he answered, "Do not fear, for those who are with us are more than those who are with them." Then Elisha prayed and said, "O LORD, I pray, open his eyes that he may see." And the LORD opened the servant's eyes and he saw; and behold, the mountain was full of horses and chariots of fire all around Elisha.

For Israel this was a time when the Arameans were planning to attack them with their armies. But the king of Aram was thwarted in the effort. More than once or twice he laid plans to attack Israel. He would make his camp, with a great army, including horses and chariots, but the king of Israel always seemed to know where his army was, and avoided the attacks. He was angered by this and gathered his servants (probably his inner circle) and made the accusation that one of them was a spy for the king of Israel. One of his servants had the courage to speak up, and told him that the prophet Elisha was telling the king of Israel all of his plans, even down to what he had been saying in his bedroom! So the king of Aram sent his spies out to find Elisha. When he was told that Elisha was in Dothan, he sent his whole army there to capture Elisha. Now that's where we see the servant getting so upset, and Elisha having the LORD open his eyes so that he could see the army of fire protecting Elisha. When the army of fire came down to Elisha, he asked the LORD to strike the whole Aramean army with blindness, which God did! Then Elisha led the blinded army to Samaria, and into the presence of the king of Israel. He then asked the LORD to open their eyes, and when their vision was restored, they were right in the middle of the capital city of the Israelites, undoubtedly surrounded by the army of Israel. The king of Israel wasn't sure what to do; he was inclined to kill them all. But before doing that he asked Elisha what he should do. Elisha told him to feed them well and send them on their way. Bottom line: Aram quit trying to attack Israel, and stayed out of the Israelite territory.

One calm prophet, one freaked out servant. What was the difference?

This is a great story of the LORD's protection of Israel. But our focus is on the day that the Aramean army was in Dothan, surrounding Elisha. When Elisha's servant saw the army he was very frightened. He asked Elisha, "What are we going to do?" Elisha seemed calm, not perturbed at all: one calm prophet, one freaked out servant. What was the difference?

Elisha was a man of God, a prophet who spoke words from God and performed many miracles. He wasn't a spy or a battle strategist. God revealed to him what the king of Aram was doing, and Elisha kept the king of Israel informed. As a man of God he was close to God, and could sense, understand and walk in the spiritual dimension. So on that morning he saw the Aramean army in the physical dimension, while he also saw the LORD's army of fire in the spiritual dimension. He could confidently declare to his servant that the forces with them were greater than the forces with the enemy. This Old Testament prophet had enough of a relationship with the LORD, and had the Spirit of God so close to him, that he was a spiritual dimension functionary. His mind was set on the things of the spiritual dimension.

Elisha's servant presents a different picture. I cannot know for sure if this attendant of the Lord was the same one mentioned earlier in II Kings: Gehazi by name. I think he was the same attendant mentioned in II Kings 4:42-44. When Elijah was brought a first fruits offering of 20 barley loaves and a bag with ears of grain, he instructed his attendant to feed it to the people. A practical man, the servant could not see these offerings feeding even a hundred men, so he hesitated and questioned the prophet. The prophet assured him that the LORD would feed everyone and there would be leftovers. The servant did not walk in the faith that Elisha had. In II Kings chapter five we are told the story of Naaman, the captain of the army of the king of Aram. He had leprosy and was cured by obeying the instructions of Elisha to wash seven times in the Jordan River. He then offered to reward Elisha, but Elisha turned this down. After he left, Elisha's servant Gehazi ran after Naaman, told lies, and received two talents of silver and two changes of clothes as gifts from him. When Elisha confronted him, he lied to Elisha's face. Elisha knew exactly what had happened, and pronounced that Naaman's leprosy would be on Gehazi and his descendants. This servant had a problem with greed and coveting. He didn't even realize that Elisha was so tuned into God's Spirit and the spiritual dimension that he would know what the servant was doing in secret. Gehazi did not walk in the "spiritual dimension mindset" of Elisha, who was indifferent to the things of the earth. At the least we can say that Elisha's servant had a mind set on the things of the physical dimension. That is why he was so fearful when the army of the Arameans surrounded them.

> We need His help to "open our eyes," to see
> what is happening in real time,
> in the spiritual dimension.

Open his eyes that he may see. What I want to point out here is that Elisha did not pray that the army of fire would be manifested in the physical dimension. Instead he prayed that his servant's eyes would be open to see! The servant needed God's help to see with his spiritual dimension vision, and that is exactly what God did. We, as Christians, often ask the Lord to show us something in the physical dimension. The song, "Come Jehovah and manifest your glory in this place" is an appeal for God to show Himself in the physical dimension. Instead we need to understand that the LORD and whatever He is doing is clear and real in the spiritual dimension. We don't need Him to manifest something; instead we need His help to "open our eyes," to see what is happening in real time, in the spiritual dimension. The song, "Open our eyes, Lord. We long to see Jesus...Open our ears, Lord, and help us to listen," is far more appropriate to what God wants, what we need, and what we should be asking for. Lord, help us to use our spiritual dimension eyes and ears to see what is really important: the spiritual dimension!

Chapter Twelve

PRINCE OF THE POWER OF THE AIR

What is Satan's position and authority in the physical dimension and in the spiritual dimension?

Luke 4:5-7 – And he led Him up and showed Him all the kingdoms of the world in a moment of time. And the devil said to Him, "I will give you all this domain and its glory, for it has been handed over to me, and I give it to whomever I wish. Therefore if You worship before me, it shall all be Yours." Jesus answered him, "It is written, 'You shall worship the Lord your God and serve Him only.'"

Just before beginning his public ministry, Jesus, full of the Holy Spirit, was led around by the Spirit in the wilderness for forty days being tempted by the devil. He overcame those temptations, and Scripture says the devil left Him until an opportune time. In the interaction between Satan and Jesus during the second recorded temptation, Satan states that all the domain of the physical dimension has been given to him, and he gives it to whomever he wishes. Is that true? Many people read this and accept it at face value. But remember this is Satan talking. Yes, this is Scripture, and the word of God is infallible. So the fact that Satan said this is true. But it does not follow that just because Satan said it makes the content true.

John 8:44 – You are of your father the devil, and you want to do the desires of your father. He was a murderer from the beginning, and does not stand in the truth because there is no truth in him. Whenever he speaks a lie, he speaks from his own nature, for he is a liar and the father of lies.

Satan said two things: all the domain of the earth had been given to him, and he could give it to whomever he wanted to. He is a liar and the father of lies, and he was lying when he spoke this temptation to Jesus. He put his own twist on this. The earth belongs to God, and He has not ever given Satan all the domain of the earth.

Psalm 24:1 – The earth is the LORD's, and all it contains, the world, and those who dwell in it.

It is true that man's sin has opened up humanity and the world to Satan's dominance. When humans sin they do give Satan a place to stand and deceive them. But not every human is under the deceptive dominance of Satan, so not all the domain of the earth has been given to him. Even before the New Covenant had God dwelling inside His people, He had people in the Old Testament that were not under the domain or control of Satan. Satan also said he could give it (the domain of the earth) to whomever he wished. That has never been true! God owns everything, and has never given the fallen Satan authority over anything. Because of the sin of mankind, Satan had rule over all the world he could deceive, in the sense that sin gives him deceptive dominance and control. But he could never do whatever he wanted. Only God can give it to whomever He wants.

John 12:28-32 – "Father, glorify Thy name." There came therefore a voice out of heaven: "I have both glorified it, and will glorify it again." The multitude therefore, who stood by and heard it, were saying that it had thundered; others were saying, "An angel has spoken to Him."

Jesus answered and said, "The voice has not come for My sake; but for your sakes. Now judgment is upon the world; now the ruler of this world shall be cast out. And I, if I be lifted up from the earth, will draw all men to myself.

When Jesus was lifted up on the cross and died for the sins of all mankind Satan was cast out. The phrase "ruler of this world" does not mean Satan rules the earth or physical dimension. Rather it refers to the idea of ruling or influencing men. The meaning of "cast out" here is the sense of banishment, or being prohibited from harming someone. Every person could have life and direct access to God through the grace, salvation of forgiveness of our Savior. And that salvation carries with it protection from Satan and his demons.

John 16:8-11 – And He, when He comes, will convict the world concerning sin and righteousness and judgment; concerning sin, because they do not believe in Me; and concerning righteousness, because I go to the Father and you no longer see Me; and concerning judgment, because the ruler of this world has been judged.

He was banished from control and dominion over any person who accepted Christ as Savior and Lord.

After the salvation work of Jesus on the cross, the New Covenant was established through His blood. Satan somehow thought that having Christ crucified would be his greatest victory over God and give him absolute control over all mankind. But instead it was his greatest defeat. He was banished from control and dominion over any person who accepted Christ as Savior and Lord. When a person becomes a Christian, the Holy Spirit dwells inside of them, reminding, convincing and convicting them of the reality that Satan is defeated and has no power over them any longer. Never forget that Satan is a judged and defeated foe because of the cross of Christ, and he no longer has any position or power over you! So don't let him take it!

II Corinthians 4:3 – And even if our gospel is veiled, it is veiled to those who are perishing, in whose case the god of this world has blinded the minds of the unbelieving so that they might not see the light of the gospel of the glory of Christ, who is the image of God.

There is a distinction in Satan's functioning toward mankind, after the cross of Jesus Christ. He loses all position and power over everyone that becomes a Christian, because they are covered and protected by the Holy Spirit within them. But everyone who has not become a Christian does not have the Holy Spirit within them, and Satan can still work his position and power of deception over them. It is the sin of man that gives Satan his position and opportunity in their lives. So he does his best to deceive and blind them, so that they do not perceive the salvation that Jesus offers. In that sense he is the god of this world over all who are not in Christ.

Ephesians 2:1, 2 – And you were dead in your trespasses and sins, in which you formerly walked according to the course of this world, according to the prince of the power of the air, of the spirit that is now working in the sons of disobedience. Among them we too all formerly lived in the lusts of our flesh, indulging the desires of the flesh and of the mind, and were by nature children of wrath, even as the rest.

Paul reminds Christians that before they had accepted Christ, because of their trespasses and sins, because of sin, they were dead. They had been living under the prince of the power of the air. This phrase doesn't mean that Satan fills the atmosphere. Rather it refers to a strong influence or presence. We might say something like this: "The air was so thick with expectancy that you could almost smell it." Satan was so strong an influence that it was almost like he was in the air all around them. Even now people who reject Jesus Christ walk in disobedience, and have twisted spirits and souls that do what Satan wants, and are headed to a bad ending in wrath and death. Satan is the prince of the power of the air to all who are not in Christ Jesus.

I John 4:4 – You are from God, little children; and have overcome them; because greater is He who is in you than he who is in the world.

We Christians are reminded that Satan is in the world; he may have influence and power over men who are not Christians, but that's not us. From the moment we accept Jesus as our Savior and Lord, God is inside of us. Therefore we have over-come Satan! It's simple math: God is greater than Satan and He is in you!

I John 5:18, 19 – We know that no one who is born of God sins; but He who was born of God keeps him, and the evil one does not touch him. We know that we are of God, and that the whole world lies in the power of the evil one.

Satan is a liar, and he will try to get us to believe that he can harm us. He wants us to believe that if we try to oppose him in the spiritual dimension, he will damage us; both in the spir-itual and physical dimensions. When we believe that Satan can still "get us," we stop doing what we are supposed to do, out of fear. We need to be reminded: Jesus Christ keeps us and Satan cannot touch us. That's the truth, and it is the path to spiritual victory.

So back to the question of Satan's position and authority. Satan is a fallen angel; created by God and living in rebellion. He does have authority over some fallen angels and humans:

the ones who buy into his lies and submit to him. His only position in God, is one of a created being in rebellion. In this day and age, under the New Covenant, Satan has no position or authority over Christians. He may trick us and deceive us, but that's why we need to be on guard with the truth of God's Word and the Truth within us. Remember, these truths are keys to the kingdom! With regard to non-Christians, because of their sin, they have given Satan a position and power in their lives. So he can touch them, even possess them and compromise their will. But if they choose to accept the Lord Jesus Christ, they can be delivered from any position, power or authority of Satan. That's the only way to have full protection from the devil.

Chapter Thirteen

THE DEVIL'S BATTLE PLAN

When we accepted Jesus Christ as our Savior and Lord, God began living inside of us (John 14:17, 17:23). It's a concept that is difficult for us to understand, but the Holy Spirit is inside of us, and we have a "born again" spirit. When Jesus died on the cross and rose from the dead, Father God rewarded him with the ultimate position of power in the spiritual dimension, seated at His right hand (Eph.1:20, 21). And Jesus gave us that same position of power and authority! (Eph. 2:6). So when we are in the spiritual dimension, Christ is with us, in us, and we have the position of authority and power, far above all rule and authority and power and dominion. Satan and his followers lose every time we confront them. That being said, Satan does not want to battle us in the spiritual dimension because he loses every time. But if he can keep us from getting to our position, maybe he can win. He tries to distract or divert us from the battlefield in the heavenlies. He will try to get us to do battle in the physical dimension. He will try anything to keep us from functioning in the spiritual dimension. Deception, Distraction, Diversion...anything to keep us off the real battlefield!

John 8:44 – You are of your father the devil, and you want to do the desires of your father. He was a murderer from the beginning, and does not stand in the truth because there is no truth in him. Whenever he speaks a lie, he speaks from his own nature, for he is a liar and the father of lies.

John 14:6 – I am the way, and the truth, and the life; no one comes to the Father but through Me.

In a recent prayer meeting, the Holy Spirit gave me a word to share with a brother, who was struggling with communication and relationship. "In your conversations and interactions, remember that if it's a lie, it's the devil and if it's the devil, it's a lie. Also if it's the truth, it's the Lord and if it's the Lord, it's the truth." Satan is a liar and the Father of lies. Any time he speaks, it is a lie. Sometimes he will state a truth, and then give it a little twist, and it becomes a lie. When he spoke to Eve in the garden he put just enough twist on what God had said to make it a lie: "You will be like God…" When he tempted Christ in the wilderness he lied when he said, "for it has been handed over to me, and I give it to whomever I wish." Satan may just tell you a bold face lie, but more often he just twists the truth enough to make it a lie. If he can deceive you, he can slow you down or neutralize your effect. Remember: if he's saying anything about what he can do, or what you cannot do, it's a lie.

Hitting our physical body. In the course of praying for people, I have heard many statements about Satan hurting someone's body.

> "Satan is making me sick."

> "The devil is attacking my body."

> "I was healed, but Satan brought it back again."

The whole idea that Satan can harm our physical bodies is a lie from the devil. The atonement of the cross of Christ gives us both salvation for our soul and healing for our bodies. And

God inside of us does not give the devil permission to touch our physical bodies. But if we think Satan can harm our physical bodies, he can trick us and hurt us. The antidote to this deception is the truth, and the truth will protect you and set you free. He whom the Son sets free is free indeed.

Getting us to fight flesh and blood. We often feel that people are opposing or attacking us. If someone is spreading lies or gossip about us, we feel that we need to set the record straight. We spend time fighting verbally with them, or spreading our version of the truth. Much effort can be put into fighting slander or scandal. But that takes our efforts and energy away from the more important spiritual dimension. We see political organizations or special interest groups as the enemy, and we end up pouring our energy and finances into opposing those groups or organizations. More effort and resources can go into politics or social movements: picketing abortion clinics or counter-picketing some demonstration that we don't agree with. This type of thing is a diversion that Satan uses to keep us from the real contesting and wrestling match against him and his followers in the spiritual dimension. Don't fight against people! Don't fight against flesh and blood in the physical dimension. Don't let Satan divert you from the real battle in the spiritual dimension. If he can keep you busy, away from the battle field, he can accomplish some of his evil plans for mankind.

When the "fight or flight" response kicks in,
Satan wants you to choose "flight" out of fear;
but God wants you to choose "fight" out of faith.

Getting us to walk in fear. God never wants us to have fear, but if Satan can get us to be afraid, he can neutralize us. The first time you sense Satan or one of his followers in the spiritual dimension, it may give you the "willies." When the "fight or flight" response kicks in, Satan wants you to choose "flight" out of fear; but God wants you to choose "fight" out of faith. You see, having a healthy fear, reverence and respect for God is appropriate.

Psalm 111:10 – The fear of the LORD is the beginning of wisdom; a good understanding have all those who do His commandments. His praise endures forever.

But there is no basis whatsoever for us to fear Satan or his demons. We have God inside of us, and we share with Him the position of ultimate power and authority over Satan and his demons in the spiritual dimension. There is no reason for us to fear the devil.

Proverb 3:25 – Do not be afraid of sudden fear nor of the onslaught of the wicked when it comes; For the LORD will be your confidence and will keep your foot from being caught.

Understand that out of His great love for us, we are delivered from all fear, and we can love all men, even as Christ loves all men and gave up his life for all. Fear can take root in the emotional part of our soul. We need to combat that with the intellectual part of our soul. There was a reason that Jesus said, "You shall know the truth, and the truth shall set you free." Use your mind. The knowledge of God's word will settle your soul, and His perfect love will drive out all fear. Have faith in God and His word, and walk with confidence and power in the spiritual dimension.

II Timothy 1:7 – For God hath not given us the spirit of fear; but of power, and of love, and of a sound mind. (KJV)

I John 4:18, 19 – There is no fear in love; but perfect love casts out fear, because fear involves punishment, and the one who fears is not perfected in love. We love because He first loved us.

Faith will trump fear every time. So Satan does not attack truth directly. But he will attack your faith subtly. His method of attack is the use of doubt. When the devil tempted Eve in the Garden of Eden, he sowed doubt to attack her faith, and then sowed deception to attack God's truth.

Genesis 4:1-5 – Now the serpent was more crafty than any beast of the field which the LORD God had made. And he said to the woman, "Indeed, has God said, 'You shall not eat from any tree of the garden'?" The woman said to the serpent, "From the fruit of the trees of the garden we may eat; but from the fruit of the tree which is in the middle of the garden, God has said, 'You shall not eat from it or touch it, or you will die.'" The serpent said to the woman, "You surely will not die! For God knows that in the day you eat from it your eyes will be opened, and you will be like God, knowing good and evil."

Satan started by questioning what God said. "Did God really say?" He sowed the seeds of doubt. It immediately affected Eve, because in her response she added words to what God said. God never said anything about touching the tree in the middle of the garden. When Satan had her doubting what God said, and putting words in God's mouth, then he flat out contradicted what God said: "You won't die! You will be like God." Satan wants us to doubt because if we doubt, then we start to question the truth of God. That erodes our faith, and presto, decreasing faith leads to increasing fear. Don't let this happen! The first moment that Satan questions what God has said, rebuke him in the name of the Lord Jesus Christ, embrace God's truth to increase your faith and move on.

Getting us to believe lies. Here are some of the big lies he tries to get us to believe, so that we quit the field before we even get into battle on the true spiritual dimension battle field.

Lie #1 – The devil can harm you in the physical dimension if you cross him. He will make you sick, or steal your possessions. Christians look at the Old Testament book of Job, where God allowed Satan to impact Job's possessions, then his health. Let's address this head on: the story of Job is not given to us to teach us how Satan can attack. Rather God chose in a special way to use Job's life as a prophetic illustration, to teach us what deep, grounded faith really is. The story of Job was never intended to be an illustration of Satan's power over God's people. In the New Covenant, we Christians are promised an abundant life and protection from the devil harming our body or possessions. Don't believe Satan's deception in this area: have faith in the truth and the truth will set you free.

I John 5:18 – We know that no one who is born of God sins (continues walking in sin); *but He who was born of God* (Jesus Christ) *keeps him, and **the evil one does not touch him.***

Fear not! Satan cannot harm you in the physical dimension when you cross him. So go ahead and fight him!

Lie #2 – Demons can take you over (demon possession) and control you. This is not true! Unfortunately Christians have been fooled by the devil, and taught falsely by some Christian leaders that they can be demon-possessed, and must have special "deliverance" ministry to be set free. There is a lot in the New Testament about humans being demon possessed, and either Jesus Christ or one of his disciples is shown casting the demons out. There is not one example of a Christian being possessed by the devil or a demon. The best "deliverance" ministry is the cross of Jesus Christ: it delivers from sin, death and the devil.

There are times that Christians are "oppressed" or "touched" by Satan or his demons. But that is only because he has deceived them into believing he can harm them. Don't let Satan deceive you! There have been times in my Christian past when I have walked in fear of the devil, and he has really hassled me. But that is no longer true, because God helped me see the truth. Satan has no right or power to oppress or touch me. He whom the Son sets free is free indeed. Let that be you!

Lie #3 – Satan and his demons can harm you in the spiritual dimension. There are a great many Christians who want to leave the spiritual dimension battle in the hands of the Lord. They are content to do their best to walk in the ways of the LORD in the physical dimension, and leave the spiritual dimension battle to others. Perhaps they have felt or seen demons, and it can be very scary! It's easier to close your spiritual eyes, or run and hide. Here's the problem. Satan is delighted when you try to ignore him, or run and hide; but Jesus wants you to "man up" and be the warrior He intended that you be. Satan and his demons cannot harm you. So get in touch with the Spirit within you, and follow your Lord into battle.

We are not qualified to fight in the spiritual dimension based on anything we do.

Lie #4 – You are disqualified. You don't know the Word of God. You don't pray enough. You aren't an experienced fighter. You have committed sins and are disqualified. It is true that knowledge of God's Word helps us better understand the spiritual dimension. And the more we pray, the better we sense the spiritual dimension. As with any skill, the more we do it, the more experienced we become. And remember: if we commit sins we have an Advocate with the Father – Christ Jesus the righteous. He does not remember our sins against us, but instead strengthens us to live and walk in victory. Here's the strongest point I want to make. We are not qualified to fight in the spiritual dimension based on anything we do: not our knowledge of the Bible; not our length of time in prayer; not our experience in spiritual things; not our righteous works or lack of sin. We are only qualified on the basis of what Christ has done. Because He died on the cross and rose from the dead, He now lives inside of us, and He now has the ultimate position and power in the spiritual dimension, which He has chosen to share with us! We can't be disqualified because He is the One who qualifies. Accept it by grace and faith, and battle man, battle!

Don't let Satan keep you from the real battlefield. If you will embrace Jesus Christ inside of you, He is the truth and will guard your heart and soul from the deceptions, distractions and diversions of Satan. The devil is the father of lies and there is no truth in him. Don't allow him to bamboozle you!

Chapter Fourteen

BATTLE IN THE HEAVENLIES

Ephesians 6:12 – For our struggle is not against flesh and blood, but against the rulers, against the powers, against the world forces of this darkness, against the spiritual forces of wickedness in the heavenly places.

We want to be strong Christians and do the best we can for God, furthering His kingdom and His righteousness. We want to say what He wants us to say, be what He wants us to be, and successfully complete the ministry He wants us to do. But so often, it seems like we are spinning our wheels fighting against other people, movements and people groups that oppose us or God. When the Apostle Paul wrote about our battle and our strengths, he spelled out the value of God's full armor for us. In the midst of that description, he pointed us in the direction of our true struggle. The Greek word translated "struggle" here refers to a contest or wrestling match where one turns and twists and does whatever he needs to do in order to win the match. The King James Version translates it as wrestling, and that sounds more positive than struggling. Our struggle takes place in the "heavenlies" – the spiritual dimension. We struggle against powers, against world forces of this darkness, against spiritual forces. Because we are so earthly minded (focused on the physical dimension) we fight against people and powers in the physical dimension, when our real battle, should be in the spiritual dimension, against Satan and the demons.

Ephesians 3:8-10 (Paul was given this grace and ministry to preach and to bring to light God's mystery ...) so that the manifold wisdom of God might now be made known through the church to the rulers and the authorities in the heavenly places.

Angels exist primarily in the spiritual dimension. They can manifest themselves in the physical dimension, but God created them as spiritual dimension dwellers. Satan and his demons are fallen angels, so they exist primarily in the spiritual dimension. Within the "fallen angels" group, there are rulers and authorities (kind of like demon generals, captains, sergeants, etc.). Satan and his demons actually believe that they are going to win against God! Satan is a liar and the Father of lies; consequently he and the demons believe lies about God, about mankind, and about what is really going to happen. Now we, as the church, make known the manifold wisdom of God to the rulers and authorities in the spiritual dimension. That most definitely includes Satan and his demons. Why is it important that Satan and his demons know the manifold wisdom of God? Is it so that they can be saved? No. Is it so that they can know the truth and the truth will set them free? No. Then what is this all about? I believe that declaring the truth of how God administers His mystery of human salvation is a weapon we wield to defeat the enemy in the spiritual dimension. When we speak the truth of the gospel the demons are struck down, defeated, and have to flee! Maybe you were thinking that we should have some kind of special Jedi sword to fight demons. Well we do have! It is the declaration of the gospel truth of God!

II Corinthians 10:3-5 – For though we walk in the flesh, we do not war according to the flesh, for the weapons of our warfare are not of the flesh, but divinely powerful for the destruction of fortresses. We are destroying speculations and every lofty thing raised up against the knowledge of God, and we are taking every thought captive to the obedience of Christ,...

We are giving the devil a body slam in the spiritual dimension, and winning the wrestling match!

Here Paul reminds us again that our real battle takes place in the spiritual dimension. When we make war, we don't use plans and strategies that work in the physical dimension, and we don't use the weapons that work in the physical world. It's a whole new ballgame, and the good news is that our spiritual dimension weapons are "powered by God." These spiritual weapons destroy the fortresses of speculation and lofty thoughts, for these thoughts and speculations, whether from Satan or created by the minds of some men, are absolutely untrue... absolutely lies! What are these spiritual weapons that are so powerful? They are the straightforward, bold declaration of the truth of the gospel of Christ! Put simply, we don't need fiery rhetoric, automatic weapons or light sabers to wrestle with and defeat Satan and his demons. We need the clear expression of the salvation that Jesus Christ has provided for all mankind by dying on the cross. Every time we witness to our neighbor, every time we tell someone at work about Jesus, every time the pastor gives an altar call at the conclusion of the service, and we all pray the sinner's prayer together, we are giving the devil a body slam in the spiritual dimension, and winning the wrestling match!

Now there are distinct times when God does all the fighting…..

Exodus 14:13, 14 – Do not fear! Stand by and see the salvation of the Lord which He will accomplish for you today; for the Egyptians whom you have seen today, you will never see them again forever. The Lord will fight for you while you keep silent.

When the children of Israel fled from Egypt, they were pursued by the Egyptian army. They came up against the Red Sea, and it appeared there was no escape. Then through Moses God miraculously parted the waters of the sea, so that all the Israelites could pass through on dry land. When the army of Egypt went into the sea on dry land to pursue them, God brought the waters back together to destroy that whole army. It was a clear case of God's people standing and waiting, and God doing all the fighting.

II Chronicles 20:17 – You need not fight in this battle; station yourselves, stand and see the salvation of the LORD on your behalf, O Judah and Jerusalem.

The nation of Judah under their king, Jehosaphat, was invaded by a large army, consisting of Moabites, Ammonites and Meunites. The king and his people were very fearful and called upon God to help them. Through the prophet Jahaziel God answered that He would take care of it. When the Israelites went out to check the camp of the enemy, they found that they had all turned on one another and killed each other. It took the Israelites three days to carry off all the plunder that was left in the camp of the enemy. This was another clear case of God's people standing and waiting, and God doing all the fighting.

But God does not intend for us to stand still every time and let Him do all the fighting in the spiritual dimension. It is typical of us that when we are aware of the spiritual dimension, we are filled with fear, but we have no reason to be afraid. God intends us to dwell in the spiritual dimension, and since He is inside of us at all times, and all around us in the spiritual dimension, we need not fear. First and foremost, He is the greatest, strongest, most powerful force across all dimensions, and He fully protects us at all times from without and within. Secondly, there are distinct times that He will carry the full load of the battle, while we stand by and enjoy the view. Thirdly, when we are to do battle, we are greater than any principalities or powers because He is with us and within us, so in the name of the Lord Jesus Christ we will win!

God has a specific, step by step plan for our activity in the spiritual dimension, and we need to live and move and have our being in the spiritual dimension, just as we do in the physical dimension.

Psalm 37:23 – The steps of a good man are ordered (prearranged, fixed, step by step, ordained) *by the Lord; and He delighteth in his way."*

We are to battle in the heavenlies against Satan and his demons. God has chosen for us to do that, and He has given us the authority and the power in the spiritual dimension to be the wrestling, battling winners. Charge!

Chapter Fifteen

GROANING TO BE CLOTHED

II Corinthians 5:1-4 – For we know that if the earthly tent which is our house is torn down, we have a building from God, a house not made with hands, eternal in the heavens. For indeed in this house we groan, longing to be clothed with our dwelling from heaven, inasmuch as we, having put it on, will not be found naked. For indeed while we are in this tent, we groan, being burdened, because we do not want to be unclothed but to be clothed, so that what is mortal will be swallowed up by life.

Philippians 1:21-24 – For to me, to live is Christ, and to die is gain. But if I am to live on in the flesh, this will mean fruitful labor for me; and I do not know which to choose. But I am hard-pressed from both directions, having the desire to depart and be with Christ, for that is very much better; yet to remain on in the flesh is more necessary for your sake.

Since his conversion to Christianity, Paul had experienced a tough life. He had been so zealous to persecute Christians, that for many years after his conversion, church people did not trust him. He gave up a prosperous, prominent life as a Jewish leader, and went on a life-long crusade to spread the truth of the gospel of Jesus Christ. That meant that he had a lot of enemies: Jews and Gentiles. In carrying out that crusade he labored hard, never getting his living from the gospel. He was often imprisoned, and the prisons in the first century were no picnic! He was beaten so often that he couldn't count how many times it had been done. On five occasions he received the terrible beating with thirty-nine lashes. We don't know for sure whether it was the Jews or the Romans who gave him the thirty-nine lashes. The Jews usually left it to the Romans to merit out the thirty-nine lash punishment. With the Romans, they used a scourge that usually had small lead weights and/or pieces of bone tied in to the straps. The idea was that forty or more lashes were a death sentence, so thirty-nine lashes stopped just short of killing the man. The bones would tear out bits of flesh and the lead weights would make bruises and contusion on the muscles. Three times he was beaten with rods. Once he was stoned. Any of these events could have killed him. On three occasions he was ship-wrecked; once he actually floated around in the sea for a day and a half! He was often in danger of dying. Almost constantly traveling in his mission and crusade, he faced dangers from rivers and seas, robbers, fellow Jews, Gentiles of many countries, and from so-called Christian brethren; dangers in the city, dangers in the wilderness. It was a hard physical life: labor and hardship, sleepless nights, often cold and exposed, sometimes hungry and thirsty without any food. Paul treasured the great spiritual dimension rewards, with thousands becoming Christians, but his existence in the physical realm was really tough. It all takes a toll on your body, and I imagine he had a lot of aches and pains all the time.

This tough existence in the physical dimension birthed a desire in Paul to depart the earth and join Christ in the spiritual dimension. Living in the physical dimension gave him the reward of winning people for Jesus Christ, so he could say, "To live is Christ!" But he was torn between staying with his primary position of physical existence and suffering all those consequences, or graduating to his eventual position of spiritual existence, and shedding the physical suffering for spiritual existence with Christ, wherein he would be able to say, "To die is gain!" It truly was a hard decision.

One night she went to sleep in a comfortable position with her arms crossed lightly on her chest.

I have been with more than one older Christian when they have been close to death. For some they reached a point where they had no more desire to stay in their failing bodies. They wanted to move on to be with the Lord. My own mother reached a point where she indicated she was having an ongoing discussion (she used the word argument) about when He was going to let her move on. One night she went to sleep in a comfortable position with her arms crossed lightly on her chest. The next morning that's exactly how they found her – dead and moved on. For these older Christians they felt they had run their race and finished their course. For Paul it was not that simple. He could still see that there was more of the earthly mission to complete. He decided he was still needed in the physical dimension to minister to Christians and non-Christians. But it was a hard decision. His body was groaning with suffering, and he was groaning with impatience and anticipation.

You see, as Christians we exist in both dimensions; the physical one and the spiritual one. Because our bodies are physical, and we have practiced all our lives to be in the world and to sense everything in that physical dimension, we are really good at perceiving physical things. When we die, we will be given a new kind of body by God; a body that is not physical but spiritual in nature. It follows that we will then be able to sense everything in the spiritual dimension much more easily. When we are in our heavenly bodies, our spiritual dimension existence is going to be easier, and seeing-sensing-perceiving things in the spiritual dimension will also come easier.

That's great for then, but what about now? We're alive in our physical bodies and we want to be for a long time. But since we are also spiritual beings, we want to exist in the spiritual dimension with all the knowledge and power that we are supposed to have, according to God's Word. So we really have to work hard with our spirit and soul to be aware of the spiritual dimension. Thankfully we have the Holy Spirit inside of us to help us see and perceive the spiritual dimension.

I Corinthians 15:50 – Now this I say, brethren, that flesh and blood cannot inherit the kingdom of God; nor does the perishable inherit the imperishable.

It will be great, "by and by in the sky." But it will be great right now if we master sensing, understanding and walking in the spiritual dimension. It's OK for us to groan for the future with our heavenly bodies, but let us also groan to be all we can be, right now, in the spiritual dimension!

Chapter Sixteen

I WAS WATCHING SATAN FALL

Luke 10:17-20 – The seventy returned with joy, saying, "Lord, even the demons are subject to us in Your name." And He said to them, "I was watching Satan fall from heaven like lightning. Behold, I have given you authority to tread on serpents and scorpions, and over all the power of the enemy, and nothing will injure you. Nevertheless do not rejoice in this, that the spirits are subject to you, but rejoice that your names are recorded in heaven."

Jesus selected seventy of His followers and sent them out in pairs, to go to the every city and place where He was going to come. He gave them instruction on what to take with them (basically nothing beyond the clothes on their back), and how to treat people who rejected them and how to stay with the people who received them. Wherever they were received in a city, they were to heal those people in it who were sick, and declare, "The kingdom of God has come near to you."

When the seventy returned to Him they were joyful. In their exuberance over the success of their mission, they exclaimed that even the demons were subject to them in the name of the Lord Jesus Christ. Jesus rejoiced with them, declaring that He had given them authority over anything that might harm them, as well as authority over the power of the enemy

(Satan). Together with them He was also full of joy and exuberance, but he reminded them that the real rejoicing shouldn't be over the spirits (demons) being subject to them, but rather that their names were recorded in heaven (because Jesus Christ was their Savior and Lord).

As he shared the joy of the seventy, He declared, "I was watching Satan fall from heaven like lightning." That is a tremendously powerful declaration. But what did He mean? For some reason scholars and commentators believe that a statement so powerful must carry a meaning far beyond the activities of the seventy.

One school of thought assigns the declaration to the initial fall of Satan. It declares that the pre-incarnate Christ was there when the prideful angel Satan rebelled against God and was cast down.

Isaiah 14:12-15 – "How you have fallen from heaven, O star of the morning (Lucifer), son of the dawn! You have been cut down to the earth, you who have weakened the nations! But you said in your heart, 'I will ascend to heaven; I will raise my throne above the stars of God, and I will sit on the mount of assembly in the recesses of the north. I will ascend above the heights of the clouds; I will make myself like the Most High.' Nevertheless you will be thrust down to Sheol, to the recesses of the pit.

Ezekiel 28:12-16 – "You were in Eden, the garden of God; every precious stone was your covering: the ruby, the topaz and the diamond; the beryl, the onyx and the jasper; the lapis lazuli, the turquoise and the emerald; and the gold, the workmanship of your settings and sockets, was in you. On the day that you were created they were prepared. You were the anointed cherub who covers, and I placed you there. You were on the holy mountain of God; you walked in the midst of the stones of fire. You were blameless in your ways from the day you were created until unrighteousness was found in you. By the abundance of your trade you were internally filled with violence, and you sinned; therefore I have cast you as profane from the mountain of God. And I have destroyed you, O covering cherub, from the midst of the stones of fire.

These two Scripture passages are prophecies against the king of Babylon (in Isaiah) and the king of Tyre (in Ezekiel). In the midst of each prophecy God speaks a strong passage against Satan himself. The words and phrases can only be applied to Satan. Scholars accept (and I agree) that each passage is referring to the fall of Satan from his created position as an angel. This fall happened before the creation of the world recorded in Genesis chapter one. Because Satan sinned in pride, he was cast down from the mountain of God; because of his sin, he had fallen down from heaven and was to be thrust down to Sheol to the pit. But is that what Christ was referring to in Luke chapter ten?

A second school of thought links the declaration to an eschatological event described in Revelation chapter 12.

Revelation 12:7-9 – And there was war in heaven, Michael and his angels waging war with the dragon. The dragon and his angels waged war, and they were not strong enough, and there was no longer a place found for them in heaven. And the great dragon was thrown down, the serpent of old who is called the devil, who deceives the whole world; he was thrown down to the earth, and his angels were thrown down with him.

Some say this describes an end time event, while others see it as a flashback to what happened to Satan when he first fell. Either way Michael and his angels wage war against the dragon and his angels, and the dragon (identified as the serpent of old, the devil) and his angels are not strong enough. So there is no longer a place found for them in heaven, and they are thrown down to the earth. Once again I ask the question: Is this what Christ was referring to in Luke chapter ten?

He saw Satan being given a fierce blow
every time a demon was cast out.

I do not believe either of these ideas applies to the words of Christ in Luke chapter ten. After looking at the context of Isaiah chapter fourteen, Ezekiel chapter twenty-eight, Revelation chapter twelve and Luke chapter ten, I believe what Christ was describing happened right then, with his disciples. The disciples, going in pairs were ministering at the different cities, just like Christ told them to do. They were healing people, casting out demons and declaring the kingdom of God; all in the name of the Lord Jesus Christ. When they returned to Jesus, they were filled with joy and marveling that even the demons were subject to them in His name. It was exciting and powerful. They lived in a time in which people feared demons, and didn't really know what to do with someone who was demon-possessed. The farther they could stay away from demon-possessed people, the better. But now, in the name of the Lord Jesus Christ, and with all the authority and power that name represented, the demons were subject to them! And Christ shared in their joy, for even though He was not present with them in the various different cities, He could see what was going on in the spiritual dimension. He saw Satan being given a fierce blow every time a demon was cast out; every time a person was healed; every time the gospel was preached! "I saw Satan fall from heaven like lightning." He didn't say that Satan could no longer be in heaven (like Revelation chapter 12). He did not say that Satan was attempting to take over God's spot (like in Isaiah chapter fourteen or Ezekiel chapter 28). What he did describe was a strong, quick vicious blow knocking Satan off his feet! He was responding to the joy and exuberance that his disciples expressed, and He was rejoicing with them in describing the negative effect upon Satan.

The same effect happens when we do battle in the name of the Lord Jesus Christ. Satan would like us to think that battle with him is a continuous wrestling match, a hand-to-hand scramble. He wants us to dread the dirty rotten scramble. If we dread it, we may fear it, and avoid it. But we need not practice avoidance! If we just minister the way Christ wants us to minister, the devil will be receiving blow after blow, and be knocked off his feet time after time. He will fall like lightning, again and again, as we sense, understand and walk in the spiritual dimension; as we confidently and forcefully move forth in the name of the Lord Jesus Christ!

Chapter Seventeen

I WAS BEING CHOKED TO DEATH!

I had been a committed Christian for seven years, married for four years, with one daughter and another one on the way. I was in the middle of my fourth year at Bible College, looking forward to graduation. I was the assistant pastor at a small church, working with the children and youth, and leading the worship in services. It was a good time, as we were moving in the direction we wanted to be going in the ministry. But something happened one day that marked and impacted my life and ministry for years afterward.

After a busy week commuting 20 miles to and from my college classes, I liked to sleep in on Saturday mornings and have a more relaxing day, before the busyness of Sunday services. As I awakened that Saturday morning I could feel someone choking me! I could feel their hands on my neck as I struggled to break free and to breathe. Someone was choking me to death! I couldn't see anyone in the room. It was a supernatural happening, and I was terrified. No matter what I tried, I could not get free. In desperation I cried out in my mind: JESUS!!

Suddenly my attacker was gone and I gasped air into my lungs. Slowly my breathing and my heart rate came back down to normal. I was convinced that Satan had attacked me, and only crying out the name of Jesus delivered me from the assault.

Now what in the world was that all about? Could Satan do that kind of thing to me whenever he wanted? Was that what it was going to be like if I moved into full time ministry? Would I be able to go to sleep again without being afraid of what I might awaken to?

Years later, when I had been a committed Christian for around forty-five years, my wife and I were at the front of our church auditorium, after the service had ended, making ourselves available to pray for people. A young Christian lady came to us and asked for prayer so that Satan would quit attacking her physically. She described marks, bruises and red marks that she would awaken with. She showed us some of the marks, and was convinced that the devil was doing it, and she needed deliverance ministry to overcome it. Now what in the world was that all about? Could Satan do that kind of thing to this young lady whenever he wanted? Was her life going to continue with these attacks? Was she going to be able to go forward in life without being afraid of what Satan might do to her body?

Job 2:1-10 – Again there was a day when the sons of God came to present themselves before the LORD, and Satan also came among them to present himself before the LORD. The LORD said to Satan, "Where have you come from? Then Satan answered the LORD and said, "From roaming about on the earth, and walking around on it." The LORD said to Satan, "Have you considered My servant Job? For there is no one like him on the earth, a blameless and upright man fearing God and turning away from evil. And he still holds fast his integrity, although you incited Me against him, to ruin him without cause." Satan answered the LORD and said, "Skin for skin! Yes, all that a man has he will give for his life. However, put forth Your hand, now, and touch his bone and his flesh; he will curse You to Your face." So the LORD said to Satan, "Behold, he is in your power, only spare his life." Then Satan went out from the presence of the LORD and smote Job with sore boils from the sole of his foot to the crown of his head. And he took a potsherd to scrape himself while he was sitting among the ashes. Then his wife said to him, "Do you still hold fast your integrity? Curse God and die!" But he said to her, "You speak as one of the foolish women speaks. Shall we indeed accept good from God and not accept adversity?" In all this Job did not sin with his lips.

This Scripture records God allowing Satan to touch Job and make him very sick with boils covering all of his body.

God had declared that Job was a blameless man who feared God and turned away from evil. Satan said that if God would allow him to make Job sick and attack his body, that Job would reject God and curse Him to His face. This Scripture records God allowing Satan to touch Job and make him very sick with boils covering all of his body. He got so sick that his wife bitterly told him to curse God and die. The good thing is that even though he was very sick, Job did not reject God or sin with his lips.

From the book of Job people have drawn the conclusion that God will allow Satan to do bad stuff to us at times. That means that Satan can attack us, at times, even damaging our bodies and making us very sick. So some people develop "deliverance" ministries to cast Satan or his demons out of us. Don't get me wrong. I do believe that we need to practice Biblical deliverance. The cross of Jesus Christ delivers us once and for all from the kingdom of darkness into the kingdom of light. If after accepting the Lord, a Christian needs deliverance from something that Satan is doing to them, they will be delivered by learning the truth and thus being set free from the deceptions of Satan.

Or some people develop teachings that our sinful conduct can leave us unprotected from Satan's attacks. Christians, who believe this kind of thing, end up spending their time fending off the attacks of Satan, instead of forcefully warring against him in the spiritual dimension. You can see why Satan wants us to believe that he can attack us like this: what better way to neutralize us before we ever get busy attacking him in the spiritual dimension?

I don't fully understand what happened to Job. I do know that the whole book shows his life as a prophecy of faithfulness toward God. I also know that things changed when Jesus Christ died on the cross for our salvation and healing. In the New Covenant God is inside of each one of us, and does not give Satan permission to touch our physical bodies!

*I John 4:4 – You are from God, little children; and have overcome them; because **greater is He who is in you than he who is in the world**.*

I John 5:18 – We know that no one who is born of God sins (continues walking in sin); *but He who was born of God* (Jesus Christ) *keeps him, and **the evil one does not touch him**.*

Luke 10:19 – Behold, I have given you authority to tread on serpents and scorpions, and over all the power of the enemy, and nothing will injure you.

I have quoted many Scriptures in the last chapters that clearly show the truth of our position and authority over Satan and his demons. Satan is a liar and the father of lies. The whole idea that Satan can harm our physical bodies is a lie from the devil. We are Christians of the New Covenant, and the atonement of the cross of Christ gives us both salvation for our souls and healing for our bodies. In the New Covenant God is inside of us, and He does not give the devil permission to touch our physical bodies or attack us. **BUT**...if we think Satan can harm our physical bodies, he can trick us and hurt us. The antidote and protection from this kind of "phony attacking" is the truth. The truth will protect you and set you free. Remember that spiritual truths are the keys to the kingdom! Memorize I John 4:4 and 5:18. Jesus gives you authority and sends you out to minister, and you have authority over all the power of the enemy: Satan. He cannot harm you! Don't allow Satan's deception to be used against you.

I will never wake up again with someone choking me to death. It was my ignorance and Satan's deception that even allowed that to happen. I now know the truth, and the truth has set me free. He whom the Son sets free is free indeed.

Chapter Eighteen

MIND SET

*Colossians 3:1, 2 – Therefore if you have been raised up with Christ, keep seeking the things above, where Christ is, seated at the right hand of God. **Set your mind on the things above**, not on the things that are on earth.*

This defines for us the best mind set to have. Set your mind on the things above, not on the things that are on earth. Christ is seated at the right hand of God in the heavenlies, that is, in the spiritual dimension. So here we're told to keep seeking and to set our minds on the things above in the spiritual dimension. We're not to set our minds on the things that are on earth, the things that are in the physical dimension.

Keep seeking the things above. There is much depth of meaning in this phrase. It means to seek and look for; to search after; to be on the watch for. It can mean trying to obtain and has the desire to possess wrapped up in it. The term was used in the legal/judicial system to mean a searching inquiry into something or someone. Before a man was to appear in front of the prefect (a high ranking authority) his background was to be thoroughly searched out, and every fact established. So to keep seeking the things above involves an intensity, a thoroughness, a tenacious action that succeeds in completion.

Set your mind on the things above. This phrase involves much more than seeking or following or checking something out. It means to point your thoughts strongly in one direction. It is used in the military sense of keeping watch or guarding. If you are on guard duty, you are fixed on defending the area you are guarding, no matter what.

Truman clubbed him with his entrenching tool.
Truman "set his mind" to successfully guard the area.

When I was in army basic training, they would put a couple of us on guard duty each night. We were responsible to walk guard around a two block area that encompassed the barracks, mess hall and HQ. We weren't allowed to carry rifles, so we would march around the area, treating our entrenching tool (small portable metal shovel) as a rifle. There was a different password each night, and we were not to allow anyone to come into the area without saying the correct password. This was all part of our training. On more than one occasion, one of the training cadre would try to bluff their way into our area without giving the password. When we recognized them as part of the HQ training cadre, and they would yell and shout their way past us, we wouldn't require them to give a password. Then we would get in trouble for failing to "guard" the area, and would have to serve KP or do 100 pushups or whatever. It was very frustrating! Well, one Sunday night one of our larger trainees, by the name of Truman, was on guard duty. One of the cadre sergeants came in late, around midnight, and he was quite drunk. He was loud and blustery, and just tried to force his way through the perimeter without giving the password. Needless to say, it didn't work. Truman clubbed him with his entrenching tool, picked him up, and took him into the HQ office, where he dumped him on the floor in front of the officer on duty, and said: "He didn't give the password." Truman turned around and marched back out to resume guard duty. The next morning, nothing was said and no one got in trouble. That was the last time any cadre tried to sneak past us without giving the password! Truman "set his mind" to successfully guard the area, and that's what he did.

Matthew 16:21-23 – From that time Jesus began to show his disciples that He must go to Jerusalem, and suffer many things from the elders and chief priests and scribes, and be killed, and be raised up on the third day. Peter took him aside and began to rebuke Him, saying, "God forbid it, Lord! This shall never happen to You. But he turned and said to Peter, "Get behind Me, Satan! You are a stumbling block to Me; for you are not setting your mind on God's interests (the things of God), *but man's."*

Here is an extraordinary exchange between Jesus and Peter that addresses the wrong mind set to have. Christ was telling his disciples beforehand of His coming arrest, death and resurrection. Peter was having none of it. He actually took Jesus to the side and rebuked Him. Peter was adamant that Jesus would not be arrested and killed. Jesus had to shock him out of his incorrect position. He said to Peter: "Get behind Me, Satan!" You see, Peter recognized that Jesus was the Messiah. Just a few verses before this exchange, Peter had made the profound declaration about Jesus: "You are the Christ, the Son of the living God." But Peter, like most of the believing Jews of his time, still believed that the Messiah would be establishing a kingdom here on earth. Therefore what Jesus was saying about being arrested and killed, just didn't fit what Peter's mind was set on. Peter's mind was set on the physical dimension and an earthly kingdom. That's what man was interested in. But God's interest was establishing His kingdom in the spiritual dimension. Our minds must be set on God's interests, on the things above, in the heavenlies, in the spiritual dimension.

Romans 8:5, 6 – For those who are according to the flesh set their minds on the things of the flesh, but those who are according to the Spirit, the things of the Spirit. For the mind set on the flesh is death, but the mind set on the Spirit is life and peace,...

We have accepted the Lord Jesus Christ as our Savior and Lord, and His Holy Spirit is inside of us. So we are now destined to be "according to the Spirit." That means doing the things He wants us to do in the way that He wants us to be doing them. We break all of our mind sets on the things of the flesh, on the things of the physical dimension. And we set our mind on anything and everything that the Holy Spirit wants. That is the mindset that brings us life and peace.

One of the things that can hinder the church in the twenty-first century is a lack of tenacity. It's easier to just go along with the flow. If things are too hard, it's easier just to give it up. There are things we know are good to hold onto, but if it's too hard, well then, we just find an easier way. An editor may say that I am using the word "easier" too often, but I am doing that on purpose. It's not easy to set our minds on the spiritual dimension, in fact it can be very hard. But it's the right thing to do. Don't just pay attention to the spiritual dimension; don't just focus on it; don't just look intently at it; don't just try hard to think about it. Set your mind tenaciously (like a bulldog that won't let go). Keep seeking until you have every fact, every truth, and every weapon. Sensing, understanding and walking in the spiritual dimension is serious business. Warriors, go forth!

Chapter Nineteen

IMAGINATION: THE KEY TO SPIRITUAL DIMENSION REALITY

Hebrews 11:1 – Now faith is the assurance of things hoped for, the conviction of things not seen.

II Corinthians 5:7 – for we walk by faith, not by sight

We know these Scriptures, and we cite them often when challenging ourselves to have faith for something. We may not see it with our physical eyes, but we can still have faith for it, in our mind's eye. We know that we know that we know we have it. And we call that faith!

I have been intrigued for years, as I have studied what psychologists say about our mind. One of the things that really got my spiritual senses going was when I came across how psychologists define imagination.

"Imagination, also called the faculty of imagining, is the ability of forming mental images, sensations and concepts, in a moment when they are not perceived through sight, hearing or other senses." (Wikipedia)

They relegated what our imagination comes up with to being "mental images," in other words, pictures in our mind that aren't real. But I was really struck by their acknowledgment that imagination functioned apart from our physical senses. The Bible teaches that faith is a function apart from our physical senses. I began asking myself if imagination was meant to be more than just a childhood development tool. Could it be that imagination could be used to perceive real things?

I have come to realize that God gave us a clear mental faculty to use in "sensing" the spiritual dimension. That faculty is our imagination. God created us with imagination, so that we could see beyond the physical dimension. His intent was that we would use it to sense real things in the spiritual dimension.

Satan is fully aware of this, and has devised deceptions and diversions, to get us to misuse or dismiss our imagination. He does this three ways:

Firstly, he has convinced us that what we see with our imagination is not real. When children are playing around with their invisible friends, we think it's cute while they are little. Years ago I took my whole family to see the movie "E.T." I think my three daughters were around six, eight and nine years old. It was an enjoyable evening. But later, in the middle of the night, one of our daughters awakened us. She was upset and afraid: E.T. was hiding in her closet! I took her back to her room, and we opened the closet together: No E.T. I assured her that she had just imagined it, and it wasn't real. We encourage our children to use their imagination because creativity is a good thing. At the same time we all know that it's just make believe. It's not real. So we train our children to grow up believing imaginary things are not real. And we were trained that way too: if we imagined it, it wasn't real. Satan wants us to believe that imagination cannot be used to perceive anything real. But some of the things we perceive with our imagination are real. They may not be in the physical dimension, but that doesn't make them any less real. Don't let Satan's lies rob you of a precious mental tool that God has given you.

Secondly, he gets us to use our imagination to think the worst has happened. Around forty years ago, I and my wife went out on a special date for our anniversary. My parents took our girls for the night, so it was just us. We had a wonderful, romantic time, getting back to our home around midnight. We found a note on our front door from our next door neighbor. It said, "Come over right way. There's a message for you." I immediately began imagining the worst: something had happened to our girls and my parents couldn't get hold of us. Jan and I rushed next door to get the message. We knocked rapidly on the door, and the neighbor finally opened up. He said, "Oh yes. This came for you." And then he handed us a beautiful bouquet of flowers. Someone had sent us lovely flowers to celebrate our anniversary! But my mind had immediately gone to imagining the worst thing had happened. That's what Satan wants us to do with our imagination, because it can increase our fear and decrease our faith, and he knows that can keep us from what God wants us to be doing. God never intended us to use our imagination to think the worst. Don't let Satan's deceptions rob you of your precious, powerful imagination.

Thirdly, he entices us to think of sin with our imagination. He tempts us to think about committing particular sins. Pornography is an obvious tool that Satan uses to get men to imagine sexual sin. We like to say that thinking it and doing it are two different things. Christ made it clear that the thoughts of sin are just as wrong as the actions of sin, when He said that when a man looks on a woman to lust after her, he has already committed adultery in his heart. The commandment tells us that we are not to covet. People who covet often see something their neighbor has and want it so much that they imagine it is theirs. Don't let Satan's enticements lead you into misusing your imagination for sin. Your God-given imagination was created for you, to accomplish far higher purposes.

God is the creator of our imagination, and He intended it for good!

In the physical dimension. The mind of man comes up with amazing designs and inventions that help us function more productively. I'm not all that ancient, but I do remember a time when homes and phone booths had phones. My first computer was a Commodore 64! I don't have to look very far at all to see how imagination has resulted in phenomenal creativity and inventiveness. My wife and I recently had the vacation of a lifetime, and spent four days in and around Paris, France. The paintings, sculptures and architecture we saw were awesome and beautiful. On more than one occasion I was open-mouthed and awestruck. These beautiful visual expressions are a phenomenal expression of people's imaginations. And think about all of the music through the generations. Composing new music is a clear function of someone's imagination.

In the spiritual dimension. The Scriptures shown at the beginning of this chapter clearly establish the first thing I will cite as a purpose for our imagination.

Imagination is the creative expression of faith.

One. Imagination is the creative expression of faith. This will absolutely set you free to walk in faith in the Lord Jesus Christ. (But that's another book for another time).

Two. God designed our imagination to be used by us in "seeing" real things in the spiritual dimension. Our imagination is a key mental tool to sense, understand and walk in the spiritual dimension. I can sense the presence of the Holy Spirit; I can identify the opponents that Jesus and I wrestle with and overcome for spiritual victory. I want you to understand that I am not talking about pretending to feel something, or see someone. I'm not talking about making something up in my mind to help my faith. I'm not talking about "confessing" something to make it so. The spiritual dimension is real. God and his angels are real. Satan and his demons are real. There are real battles happening, right now, in the spiritual dimension. None of us need to pretend these things are real. What we need is to use our God-given imagination to sense the reality of the spiritual.

There is a wonderful song that we sing in church these days, "I Can Only Imagine." I have viewed all the lyrics from MercyMe Lyrics, and my heart beats closely to Jesus every time we sing it. It is all about the future event, when the singer sees Jesus, face to face, and spends eternity with Him.

I can only imagine
When that day comes
And I find myself
Standing in the Son

I can only imagine
When all I will do
Is forever
Forever worship You
I can only imagine

What I hope is that someone with the appropriate God-given talent will someday write a song entitled, "I Can Really Imagine," about us using our imagination to sense the spiritual dimension and our Lord and Savior right now. That's what God created our imagination for, and we can use it to sense, understand and walk in the spiritual dimension.

Chapter Twenty

FUNCTIONING IN THE SPIRITUAL DIMENSION - AWARENESS

Practice Being Aware. Being aware of our physical surroundings comes automatically because we have done it all our lives. Being unaware of our spiritual surroundings comes automatically too. It may be indifference, discomfort or fear that makes it easier for us to tune out the spiritual dimension. But that doesn't mean it's not there. Because we have Jesus Christ inside of us, there is no reason to fear. The reason we are uncomfortable with the spiritual dimension is because we're not used to sensing, understanding and walking in it. It may seem that it's easier just to ignore it now, and deal with it later, but if we want to do what God wants us to do, we can't remain indifferent to the spiritual dimension. Instead we need to practice being aware.

Firstly, when you pray you start talking to God. At that moment in time you are beginning an interaction in the spiritual dimension. Stop for a moment and focus on God. You are now sensing and being aware of the spiritual dimension. As you talk to the Lord, open yourself up and realize that Jesus Christ is inside of you. Reach to Him, touch Him, embrace Him; this gives you a better feel of the spiritual dimension. Do this every time you pray, and it will help develop your spiritual senses. You are using your spiritual senses and becoming aware of the spiritual dimension.

Secondly, the next time you are in a church service (and you should be in a church service a lot – it's good for you!), I want you to go beyond the normal praise and prayer. Most of the time when we are at church, we enjoy the atmosphere, and use it to help us tune in to the Lord. We usually shut out the people and things around us, and just try to have a one-on-one with Jesus. That is good, but we need to go beyond this. So as you are focused on Jesus in your prayer and praise (I usually have my eyes closed, which helps me focus), stop and in your mind reach out to the people around you. Because you are praying or praising, you are functioning in the spiritual dimension, and the people around you who are also praying or praising are functioning in the spiritual dimension. Just be aware that you're all together. This is what it really means to be "in church." Now you are stretching beyond just yourself and God, and becoming aware of others. You're not just in your very own spiritual cocoon, but in a larger spiritual group. You are using your spiritual senses to be aware of the spiritual dimension.

Practice your awareness of the spiritual dimension, instead of ignoring it.

Do this first and second step a lot. The more you do it, the better. You want to practice your awareness of the spiritual dimension, instead of ignoring it. Just as you are in the physical dimension 24 hours a day, you are also in the spiritual dimension 24 hours a day. So be aware of it! It's good for you and good for God's kingdom.

Sensing. Since we began our existence with a physical body, we have grown up doing everything with our body. We've gotten really good at using our senses to be aware of the physical world around us. We feel everything with our sense of touch. Every time any part of our body comes in contact with some physical thing, we feel it. Our sense of smell picks up close odors, and some at a distance; some nice and some not so nice. Our sense of taste is limited to what comes in contact with the taste buds, and strongly influences our eating habits, since we tend to eat more of what has pleasurable taste, and less of what tastes badly to us. Our hearing picks up sounds for quite a distance, although there are some sounds we don't hear because our hearing is limited to a certain range (for example, we can't hear the sound of a dog whistle). With our sight we see physical things, near or far. We can't sense everything in the physical dimension because our senses are limited by range and position. But they are automatic. Touching, smelling, tasting, hearing and seeing in the physical dimension just seems to happen. That's because we have used them since birth, and we're pretty good at using them. There are times that we really need to focus (awareness), so that we get the best reception possible. For example: tasting the nuances of a good wine; eavesdropping on someone else's conversation; making out the details of some sign in the distance; using our nose and brain to figure out what an unusual smell is; identifying what an object is that we have touched in the dark. Whether we just have our senses on automatic, or we're really focusing in, we are aware of our physical surroundings because we use our senses.

Now about sensing in the spiritual dimension. There haven't been a lot of scientific studies on spiritual senses, so the ground may seem uncharted. But you'll be amazed at how obvious it is.

When Elisha prayed for his servant to be able to see the army of fire that protected them, he asked the Lord to open his eyes. When the servant saw the army of fire, he was using the spiritual sense of sight, because God opened his spiritual eyes.

When the Bible records conversations God was having, people heard Him talking. Sometimes that may have been a physically audible sound. But there are times that God speaks and people hear it with their spiritual hearing. On more than one occasion God spoke and some people heard the words, while others just thought it was thunder.

There's something else I refer to as "feeling." Have you ever heard the saying, "Someone just walked over my grave?" Or someone will suddenly feel a chill and the hairs on the back of their neck seem to stand up? People have said that they can feel it when a ghost is in the room. There have been special church services in which people say that they can feel the presence of angels. This is what I refer to as "feeling" something in the spiritual dimension.

Perhaps some of this seeing or hearing or feeling has just been something in people's minds, but not real in the spiritual dimension. They haven't made it up or lied; they may simply be interpreting a mental event as a spiritual event. But at least some of these events have been bona fide spiritual dimension happenings. Certainly the ones recorded in Scripture are absolutely real!

I want every Christian believer enabled to see what God wants them to see in the spiritual dimension. I want them to hear God and His angels with clarity and understanding in the spiritual dimension. I want them to feel other beings in the spiritual dimension, just as God wants them to. I don't want Christians to be afraid of these spiritual feelings. Because we have Jesus Christ in us, and we have a position of authority and power in the spiritual dimension, just as He does, we can be fearless in sensing, understanding and walking there.

God wants every Christian to be able to sense the spiritual dimension. There is a passage in Isaiah 30 that indicates that God wants us to turn to Him, and to long for Him. As we do this, He will be gracious to us and answer us.

Isaiah 30:21 – Your ears will hear a word behind you, "This is the way, walk in it," whenever you turn to the right or to the left.

There is nothing that compares to God's voice regularly guiding us on how to walk in His ways. We want our spiritual hearing to be finely tuned to hear Him in the spiritual dimension.

On a "works" note: Sensing the spiritual dimension does not depend upon works of righteousness. I ran across an interesting concept in Jewish tradition and training. It described our lack of sensing God's presence as similar to our ears not being able to hear radio waves. It then said that doing a mitzvah strengthens the signal of God's presence and fine tunes our spiritual senses to be tuned in to it. And when we do many mitzvot it is easier to sense God's presence and the spiritual dimension. A mitzvah is a precept or commandment; a good deed done in religious duty. What was being said is that the more commandments we obey and good deeds we do, the more we will sense the spiritual dimension. This is the classic message of religious good works, and while doing good things may put us in a more receptive mood to be aware of spiritual things, it does not earn us access. Our access to the spiritual dimension, our awareness of it, our position in it, and our sensing of it are all accomplished by the cross of Jesus Christ, and that is by His grace, not our works!

All of our lives we have practiced flipping the switch and turning off our awareness of the spiritual dimension. We would let it surface once in awhile, during a prayer or a special church service. But we always seemed to say the "Amen," or pronounce the "Benediction," and retreat into our comfort zone in the physical dimension, clicking the switch off. Ask yourself this question: If God is inside of me, is He still inside of me when I flip my "awareness" switch off? Of course He is! Well, we're ready now to practice awareness and tune our senses. It's functioning time!

Chapter Twenty-One

FUNCTIONING IN THE
SPIRITUAL DIMENSION - CONVERSATION

Conversation. My definition for prayer is any conversation that we have with God. That keeps it clear. It doesn't have to be eloquent; we don't have to be in one exact position or location. It's talking with God. It can be initiated by us or by Him, at any moment and in any place. When He initiates the conversation, it is a good thing if we can hear Him and talk.

In Genesis chapter eighteen we have an unusual conversation take place between the LORD and Abraham. The LORD appeared in an unusual way. Abraham was sitting at the door of his tent, on a very hot day, and suddenly saw three men just across from him. The context of chapters eighteen and nineteen shows that the three were two angels and the LORD. Abraham extended hospitality to the three, putting before them food and drink. The LORD gave Abraham a prophecy that within a year Sarah would bear a son to him. The three got up to leave. Then the LORD said to the angels that He should tell Abraham what He was about to do to Sodom and Gomorrah because of their great sin. Then He told Abraham. The two angels then departed, heading for Sodom. Abraham was left standing before the LORD. Abraham then spoke to the LORD and bargained with Him about not destroying Sodom if there were enough righteous men still left in the city. Will you spare the city if there are 50 righteous there? God said He would spare the city if there were 50 righteous there. Abraham kept bargaining: For 45? For 40? For 30? For 20? For 10? The LORD answered each time that He would not destroy Sodom, for the sake of 50, or 45, or 40, or 30, or 20, or 10 righteous people. After the LORD said He would spare the city for 10 righteous people, He departed and Abraham returned to his place. What a conversation! Abraham was respectful and bold at the same time, and God patiently listened and answered each time. Abraham was just sitting there, taking it easy, in the heat of the day, and the LORD showed up and initiated quite a conversation. This is an example of talking with God.

In Exodus chapters three and four we have an extraordinary conversation take place between Moses and the LORD. Moses saw a bush burning on the mountainside, and it just kept burning without being burned up. So he went to check it out. The LORD spoke to him from the burning bush, telling him to remove his shoes, since he was standing on holy ground. Then He spoke extensively about delivering the Israelites out of slavery in Egypt and bringing them to the Promised Land. He specified that He wanted Moses to lead them out. Quite a conversation then ensued, with Moses showing reluctance to do what God was telling him to do. "Not me, LORD. I'm not qualified." "What is Your name?" "What if they don't believe me?" I can't speak well." "I don't want to do it; find somebody else." God patiently answered Moses each time, even performing miracles to reassure him. Moses still didn't want to do what the LORD was telling him to do. God finally got angry and told Moses to do what he was told, and God would take care of things. What a conversation! Moses used questions and excuses to try and get out of doing what God was telling him to do. God did a lot of explaining and reassuring with miraculous signs, and finally just told Moses, "Do it!" Moses was out pasturing Jethro's flock and the LORD showed up and initiated this conversation. This is another example of talking with God.

I cite these two examples because I want to move us away from a fearful, hesitant, stumbling, brief kind of approach to the idea of having a talk with God. Abraham bargained and bargained with God. Moses dragged his feet something fierce and said he didn't want to do it. Yet God still had these conversations, and God accomplished His will. We should not be afraid to have any talk with God. There's no reason to be hesitant or stumbling: God loves us and wants to converse with us. And let's spend more time in the talk: these conversations with Moses and Abraham were lengthy and had a lot of content.

In I Samuel chapter three, we find the boy Samuel, serving the priest Eli, at the tabernacle in Shiloh. Samuel's mother Hannah had given her little boy to be a servant of the house of the LORD because God had granted her prayer and opened her womb, so she could have children. We see here an example of listening to God. Evening time had come and Eli went to bed. So did the boy Samuel. Then came the call, "Samuel!" He got up quickly, went to Eli saying, "You called me. Here I am." Eli said, "No, I didn't call you. Go back to bed." So Samuel went back to bed. Again the call came, "Samuel!" So he got up again and went to Eli. "You called me. Here I am." "No, I didn't call you. Go to bed!" Back to bed the boy went. A third time the call came: "Samuel!" He went again to Eli. This had to be getting old for Eli, and confusing for Samuel. But it finally dawned on Eli that it must be the LORD calling Samuel. So he told him to go back to bed; if the LORD calls you again, say, "Speak, LORD, for thy servant is listening."

The call came again, "Samuel, Samuel!" This time he responded just like Eli told him to: "Speak, for Thy servant is listening." God proceeded to give Samuel a long message pronouncing judgment upon Eli and his sons, because of their disobedience. This was the boy's initiation into listening to the LORD. He thought it was Eli, but when he was instructed that it was the LORD, he expressed the exact attitude we need when we talk with God: "I'm listening, Lord."

In Acts chapter nine we see Saul being pulled up short by a conversation with God. Saul opposed the Christian church and was devoting himself full time to getting Christians imprisoned and even killed. He was traveling to Damascus so he could find any Christians and bring them back to Jerusalem in chains. Suddenly a light from heaven flashed around him, and he heard a voice: "Saul, why are you persecuting Me?" Saul had fallen to the ground: "Who are you, Lord?" God responded, "I am Jesus whom you are persecuting. Go into the city and you will be told what to do." Saul got up, found he was blind, and had to be led by hand into Damascus. Wow! When God wants to speak to you, you'd better listen. It took a miracle, God's voice and blindness to get Saul to listen. Let's pick up a different lesson from this conversation. Even when Saul was heading in the wrong direction, even hurting the people of the church, God struck up a conversation with him. So also, God may speak to us even if we aren't talking to Him, or if we're flat out going in the wrong direction. Whenever He may speak to you, the best policy is to listen.

"How're you doing, Lord?"

Talk with God. Every day. All the time. Just say, "How're you doing, Lord?" It doesn't need to be fancy or profound talk. And make time to listen. Don't be so quick to get to the "Amen." Every time you do, it will increase your awareness and functioning in the spiritual dimension. And He is so good to talk to.

Praying in the Spirit. It is obvious that functioning in the spiritual dimension involves our spirit and God's Spirit inside of us, in a major way. Let's look at praying that involves our spirit and the Spirit.

Speaking in Tongues. If you do not believe that speaking in tongues is for today, you may want to skip this section. If you speak in tongues while praying, it is best to do it in private, since the Bible teaches that it is for self-edification. When we are in church we are to do things that edify everyone present. Paul says that if tongues are spoken in the church service, they should be interpreted so that everyone can understand and be built up. I Corinthians chapter fourteen gives us a lot of insight into the value of tongues. When you pray in the Spirit (speaking in tongues) you are speaking to God (14:2); you are speaking mysteries (14:2), and you build yourself up (14:4). It is a kind of praying that does take some faith, because we like to be in control of the content of what we say. In the case of praying in the Spirit, we do the speaking, but He controls the content. It is what needs to be said in the spiritual dimension, so that we are built up, and can sense, understand and walk there. While we may not understand with our minds, our spirit and soul are built up. It definitely helps us function in the spiritual dimension.

Groaning too deep for words. There is a Scripture that many Pentecostals misinterpret.

Romans 8:26, 27 – In the same way the Spirit also helps our weakness; for we do not know how to pray as we should, but the Spirit Himself intercedes for us with groaning too deep for words; and He who searches the hearts knows what the mind of the Spirit is, because He intercedes for the saints according to the will of God.

I have heard it said that these verses are referring to speaking in tongues. But the phrase "too deep for words" is literally "unutterable, or cannot be uttered." Speaking in tongues is an utterance, so that is not what is being referred to here. Rather from the deep parts of the Spirit of God, He intercedes for us. This is the only place in the New Testament where the intercession referred to is literally "super intercession." Only the Holy Spirit can help us in our prayers in such a huge way: the very deep heart and soul of God super intercedes for us. It is His groaning, not ours. I will accept that sometimes we get so deep into prayer and communion with God that we make groaning sounds. But here in Romans it is the Holy Spirit doing the groaning, not us. That's spiritual dimension dynamite, and that's how God helps us. As you pray, never fear going deeper and getting more intense. The Holy Spirit is your guard and your guide.

Conversation... Prayer... Talking with God. This is absolutely our major penetration and connection to the spiritual dimension. Don't make it a hard thing: just talk to Him, and listen. He makes it easy and He helps us do it. From the moment we accepted Jesus Christ as our Savior and Lord, He came inside of us. Now His Spirit and our spirit are inside of each of us, and there's nothing like "our spirit-His Spirit" spiritual dimension conversation. We're ready now to talk and listen – a lot – with God. It's functioning time!

Chapter Twenty-Two

FUNCTIONING IN THE SPIRITUAL DIMENSION - ACTION

Acting. We are actors, players, participants, in the spiritual dimension. And we who have trained ourselves to show love for our fellow man, acting as perfect ladies and gentlemen, must see just how different we are to be as God's army in the spiritual dimension.

Matthew 11:12 – From the days of John the Baptist until now the kingdom of heaven suffers violence, and violent men take it by force. (The kingdom of heaven is forcibly entered, and forceful men take it by force).

Luke 16:16 – The Law and the Prophets were proclaimed until John; since that time the gospel of the kingdom of God has been preached, and everyone is forcing his way into it.

Ephesians 6:12 – For our struggle is not against flesh and blood, but against the rulers, against the powers, against the world forces of this darkness, against the spiritual forces of wickedness in the heavenly places.

I have expressed that God wants us to sense, understand and walk in the spiritual dimension. But that sounds kind of tame when we look at the words Scripture uses to describe our walking there. We are His warriors and because of the position and power that He has given us in the spiritual dimension, we don't just walk there... we conquer! We are not spiritual diplomats; we don't act like gentlemen in the spiritual dimension. We are warriors!

Forceful Men. The Greek means forceful or violent men. With certain men you see a "command presence." If you have ever watched a Steven Seagal movie (like Executive Decision), he is one actor who has the "command presence" aura down to a T. Before he takes any violent action, he just walks in with that forceful aura. When forceful men walk into a room, everyone turns their attention to them. When they issue a command, people "snap to," to carry out the orders. That's what forceful men are like. Their attitude and carriage project confidence and capability. And that's how we are to act and walk. We don't sneak into the spiritual dimension; we don't tiptoe around. We use force because we are forceful. That's what is needed to enter the spiritual dimension (the kingdom of heaven is forcibly entered and forceful men take it by force).

Forceful Entry. We forcefully enter the spiritual dimension. Whatever is in the way of our getting into our God-given position and territory, we forcefully remove. Maybe it's things within us, such as sin or vain imaginations. Maybe it's the devil or his demons. We don't let anything get in our way or delay us from entering the spiritual dimension. We forcefully enter and seize our territory. Avidly, eagerly seize the heavenlies! When it comes to the spiritual dimension, we are not so much diplomatic ambassadors as we are members of the S.W.A.T. team. If we have to break the door down, then we do it!

Wrestling. This is a better translation than "struggling." The word refers to a conflict with someone in which you are contesting their every move and defeating them. You are twisting and turning, swinging around and swaying backward and forward; doing anything and everything you need to do to win. It's more like no-holds-barred combat than Greco-Roman wrestling. It is **not** a situation of winning some and losing some, like a high school wrestling match. With God inside of us, and our God-given position and power, we are to win every time.

Acting and walking in the spiritual dimension is not a stroll in the park; it's not a cake walk. It's tough, forceful wrestling and seizing of position and territory. But it's worth it, because it's what you are made for and what our Lord wants for us and for His kingdom.

Teamwork. No lone rangers in the Church. No solitary soldiers in the spiritual dimension. Jesus taught clearly that we need to work together. As a team we will succeed in everything He wants us to do. It was not accidental that He sent His disciples out two by two.

Matthew 18:19, 20 – Again I say to you, that if two of you agree on earth about anything that they may ask, it shall be done for them by My Father who is in heaven. For where two or three have gathered together in My name, I am there in their midst.

Ecclesiastes 4:9 – Two are better than one because they have a good return for their labor. For if either of them falls, the one will lift up his companion. But woe to the one who falls when there is not another to lift him up. Furthermore, if two lie down together they keep warm, but how can one be warm alone? And if one can overpower him who is alone, two can resist him. A cord of three strands is not quickly torn apart.

Jesus had just finished talking about what to do if your brother sins. From private confrontation all the way to telling it to the whole church, the goal is to get your brother to listen and deal with the sin. After this process is presented, then Jesus made a very strong statement about binding or loosing things on the earth bringing about binding or loosing things in heaven. Then we have this important team work statement about two or three. We have a tendency to practice our prayers and our spiritual dimension entries alone: going solo. God's advice is to work as a team with at least two or three together.

> Look for the simple things you can agree on,
> and then build your arsenal of agreement.

Agree on earth. If you follow some church life situations, or the postings of some church leaders on the internet, you might despair of Christians ever agreeing about anything. But it can be done. As you make your battle connections with one or two other Christians, look for the simple things you can agree on, and then build your arsenal of agreement. It is crucial that you have the unity that comes from agreement.

About anything. Let me break this up. In the physical dimension Jesus always wants us to seek first His kingdom and righteousness, and he doesn't want us to worry about our food, clothing or shelter. He knows that whatever he blesses us with in the physical dimension will be handled well by us, as faithful stewards. But now I'm talking about our successful action in the spiritual dimension. We can agree in the physical dimension about anything in the spiritual dimension.

Whatever we bind or loose on earth (physical dimension) shall be bound or loosed in heaven (spiritual dimension). He makes a wide open statement because as humans we don't think as big as God. In functioning and succeeding in the spiritual dimension, ask big for God's help and you will succeed. Sometimes we don't think big enough. What we don't understand, we make hard; what we don't understand we try to explain with our finite understanding, and that makes the things of God "smaller." **BUT GOD**...God is able to do abundantly beyond all that we ask or think, and so He uses the language of big, the language of possibilities: agree about anything and My Father will do it.

In His Name. When you get together and are ready to swing into action, call the name of the Lord Jesus Christ over your meeting, your prayer, your ministry, or whatever you are doing. When God's name is called over your activities, He releases His volitional power; He swings into action on your behalf. There is power in His name, so gather together in His name and see the victory of the Lord.

And so we are action warriors in the army of the Lord, and the fighting we do is not against flesh and blood in the physical dimension, but against Satan and his demons in the spiritual dimension. It works best when we're a team: with at least two warriors fighting back to back. We need to make our connections, assemble our teams and forcefully take our God given position in the spiritual dimension. It's functioning time!

Chapter Twenty-Three

IN THE SPIRIT ON THE LORD'S DAY

Revelation 1:9-11 – I, John, your brother and fellow partaker in the tribulation and kingdom and perseverance which are in Jesus, was on the island called Patmos because of the word of God and the testimony of Jesus. I was in the Spirit on the Lord's day, and I heard behind me a loud voice like the sound of a trumpet, saying, "Write in a book what you see, and send it to the seven churches: to Ephesus and to Smyrna and to Pergamum and to Thyatira and to Sardis and to Philadelphia and to Laodicea." Then I turned to see the voice that was speaking with me. And having turned I saw seven golden lampstands;...

John the Beloved was a Christian who sensed, understood and walked in the spiritual dimension. He was an apostolic leader in the exciting first century, as the church rapidly expanded from Jerusalem, to Judea, into the Roman Empire and beyond. John furthered the spread of the gospel, despite tribulation and persecution. For his activities he was imprisoned and exiled, on the Isle of Patmos, by the Roman authorities. This limited his range of ministry, but did not eliminate his work with the church. With all this experience and the many years of ministering in the Holy Spirit, he had become a spiritual dimension warrior. God chose to use him as the channel through which we received the book of Revelation. The Lord's Day is generally understood to be the first day of the week. Christians honored the day because Jesus rose from the dead on the first day of the week. John records that he was "in the Spirit on the Lord's Day." John knew how to immediately be in touch with the Holy Spirit inside of him. He would reach out with his spirit to touch the Holy Spirit, and it made him immediately aware of his own presence in the spiritual dimension with God.

Revelation 4:1, 2 – After these things I looked, and behold, a door standing open in heaven, and the first voice which I had heard, like the sound of a trumpet speaking with me, said, "Come up here, and I will show you what must take place after these things." Immediately I was in the Spirit; and behold, a throne was standing in heaven, and One sitting on the throne.

John had faithfully recorded the seven letters to the churches of Asia, and then the revelation took a distinct turn. He heard the same voice from chapter one: it was the Lord Jesus Christ talking to him. The Lord told him to "come up here," and He would show him "what must take place after these things." This is a pivotal point in the book of Revelation, because the letters to the churches recorded in chapters two and three were for existing churches in Asia at the moment in time that John received the revelation (between AD 80-95). But from Rev. 4:1 on, it is talking about events that were future to AD 80-95. Most people conclude that the rest of the book of Revelation is eschatological, that is, that it refers to end-time events. John was suddenly in the throne room of God in heaven. He says he was immediately in the Spirit, and it happened. John had earlier indicated that he was in the Spirit on the Lord's Day when God began speaking to him. What I think happened here, is that John got busy recording the letters to the seven churches, and as he recorded the Lord's message to those churches, he got to thinking about these particular churches and the people he knew in those churches.

Even when we are functioning in the spiritual dimension, we still use our mind, and can think about a lot of things. When he had recorded the last letter, he suddenly re-focused on the next part of the unfolding revelation. We can reach out again to touch the Holy Spirit inside of us, with our spirit. It's the same as we saw in the book of Acts. Even though the disciples were filled with the Holy Spirit on the Day of Pentecost, several more instances are recorded of them being filled with the Holy Spirit. We can reach inward with more intense effort and commune ever deeper with God's Spirit.

Revelation 17:3 – And he carried me away in the Spirit into a wilderness; and I saw a woman sitting on a scarlet beast, full of blasphemous names, having seven heads and ten horns.

The woman, also called Babylon is representative of the forces that oppose Christ and His people, and John will now see that she is judged and destroyed by God's forces of good. Here one of the seven angels carries John away "in the Spirit" to show him the downfall and destruction of the woman, Babylon. Angels can show us things in the spiritual dimension, and can take us places to see whatever God wants us to see, and to do whatever God wants us to do. In the spiritual dimension God is always inside of us, full of all power and authority, and the angels are our fellow warriors.

Revelation 21:10, 11 – And he carried me away in the Spirit to a great and high mountain, and showed me the holy city, Jerusalem, coming down out of heaven from God, having the glory of God. Her brilliance was like a very costly stone, as a stone of crystal-clear jasper.

The tremendous revelation about the end times is coming near to the end. Satan and his demons, and all humans who oppose God are cast into the lake of fire. Judgment has happened and now the new heaven and earth are revealed. One of the seven angels carries John away "in the Spirit" to a high mountain, and he gets to see the New Jerusalem coming down out of heaven from God: the ultimate renewal, the ultimate victory, the eternal purpose and plan of God. Once again with the angel's help, John is intensely focused on the spiritual dimension.

The Holy Spirit and the angels are our helpers in walking with us in the spiritual dimension.

John's experience in being given the Revelation of Jesus Christ is an extraordinary example of awareness and sensing in the spiritual dimension. It shows clearly that the Holy Spirit and the angels are our helpers in walking with us in the spiritual dimension. Now we could look at all of this phenomenal revelation and conclude that John was really special, but we're just "regular" Christians, so it's not really for us. But maybe you are like me, and hunger to have this kind of awareness and sensing and spiritual walking. Lord, open our eyes that we may see!

Chapter Twenty-Four

NO LONGER A PLACE IN HEAVEN

*Revelation 12:7-9 – And there was war in heaven, Michael and his angels waging war with the dragon. The dragon and his angels waged war, and they were not strong enough, and there was **no longer a place found for them in heaven.** And the great dragon was thrown down, the serpent of old who is called the devil and Satan, who deceives the whole world; **he was thrown down to the earth, and his angels were thrown down with him.***

This chapter is not about the present day spiritual dimension that we are to sense, understand and walk in. It is about the Great Tribulation, an end time period that is going to be terrible for humans that are present for it. It has value because it shows God's position and power while also showing Satan's cruel power over unregenerate humanity. I venture to say that I will be presenting an interpretation of Revelation chapter twelve that you have never heard before.

*Revelation 4:1 – After these things I looked, and behold, a door standing open in heaven, and the first voice which I had heard, like the sound of a trumpet speaking with me, said, "Come up here, and I will show you **what must take place after these things.***

We have a key transition point in the book of Revelation at the beginning of chapter four. The Lord commands John to "come up here," and he will be shown what must take place after these things. "These things" refers to John's present time, at the end of the first century A.D., when he recorded the seven letters to the seven churches of Asia. From chapter 4:1 on, the rest of the book of Revelation is "after these things." In other words they are in the future, after the end of the first century. That means that Revelation chapter twelve is referring to things in the future, after A.D. 80-95, when the seven letters were written. Some people have looked at the language and symbolism in chapter twelve, and assigned the events to Old Testament Israel times, or even pre-creation times. I believe that is incorrect, and that everything in Revelation chapter twelve occurs sometime after A.D. 80-95.

Revelation 12:4 – And his tail swept away a third of the stars of heaven and threw them to the earth.

Many people teach that when Satan rebelled against God and fell, he took a third of the angels with him (what we now refer to as demons). They base it on this verse: Revelation 12:4. There is no other Bible reference to this. But, once again, I point out that this verse refers to something in the future, after A.D. 80-95, and most probably a time at the end. Here we may have a quantifying (one third) of the angels of Satan that are cast down to the earth in the future battle with Michael and his angels. And it would be reasonable to say that Satan's angels that are defeated in Revelation twelve are the same angels/demons that fell with Satan way back when he first rebelled against God. So maybe Satan did take a third of the angels with him, when he rebelled against God and fell.

Revelation 12:6 – Then the woman fled into the wilderness where she had a place prepared by God, so that there she would be nourished for one thousand two hundred and sixty days.

Revelation 12:14 – But the two wings of the great eagle were given to the woman , so that she could fly into the wilderness to her place, where she was nourished for **a time and times and half a time,** *from the presence of the serpent.*

In Revelation chapter twelve, the dragon is clearly identified as Satan. The woman is a bit more of a puzzle. Some say the woman is the nation Israel, and they say it either refers to Israel in the Old Covenant, or Israel in the end times. Others say the woman is the church of Jesus Christ, either in the church age, after A.D. 80-95 or in the end time. I believe it definitely refers to the end time, because a 3 ½ year time period is referred to twice. In the book of Revelation a 3 ½ year time period is referred to several times. It is the Great Tribulation that occurs at the end of the church age. Remember that all of chapter twelve is future to A.D. 80-95, and the tie-in with the 3 ½ year Great Tribulation definitely places it in the end times.

Revelation 12:12 – For this reason, rejoice, O heavens and you who dwell in them. Woe to the earth and the sea, because the devil has come down to you, having great wrath, knowing that he only has a short time.

At the end of time, Satan and his demons are thrown out of the spiritual dimension for the 3 ½ year Great Tribulation.

So the great battle in the heavens is played out, as Michael and his angels battle and defeat Satan and his angels. There was no longer a place found for them in heaven; Satan and his angels were thrown down to the earth. At the end of time, Satan and his demons are thrown out of the heaven, the heavens, the heavenlies, the spiritual dimension, and thrown into the physical dimension (the earth). Remember that Satan and the demons are spiritual beings, created by God to primarily dwell in the spiritual dimension, although they can also interact in the physical dimension. But in the end time they are kicked out of the spiritual dimension, and limited to existence in the physical dimension for the 3 ½ year Great Tribulation. Everyone in the spiritual dimension will rejoice because Satan and the demons won't be there! Satan will first try to destroy the woman (maybe Israel, maybe the church), but the woman is protected for the 3 ½ years, and cannot be harmed by Satan. When this happens Satan will know he has only a short time, and he will wreak havoc on the entire physical dimension. Woe to the earth and the sea; because Satan knows his time is short, and with great wrath he will kill and destroy in the physical dimension. Satan and the demons were designed to be spiritual dimension beings, but they can't be there anymore. It will be terrible for mankind in that time of wrath. Remember that Satan is a murderer. That's why the Great Tribulation is described in such horrific details throughout the book of Revelation. You do not want to be there, no matter how you might glamorize the time!

Chapter Twenty-Five

NEW HEAVENS AND A NEW EARTH

Revelation 21:1-3 – Then I saw a new heaven and a new earth; for the first heaven and the first earth passed away, and there is no longer any sea. And I saw the holy city, New Jerusalem, coming down out of heaven from God, made ready as a bride adorned for her husband. And I heard a loud voice from the throne, saying, "Behold, the tabernacle of God is among men, and He will dwell among them, and they shall be His people, and God Himself will be among them...

II Peter 3:7-13 – But by His word the present heavens and earth are being reserved for fire, kept for the day of judgment and destruction of ungodly men. But do not let this one fact escape your notice, beloved, that with the Lord one day is like a thousand years, and a thousand years like one day. The Lord is not slow about His promise, as some count slowness, but is patient toward you, not wishing for any to perish but for all to come to repentance. But the day of the Lord will come like a thief, in which the heavens will pass away with a roar and the elements will be destroyed with intense heat, and the earth and its works will be burned up. Since all these things are to be destroyed in this way, what sort of people ought you to be in holy conduct and godliness, looking for and hastening the coming of the day of God, because of which **the** *heavens will be destroyed by burning, and the elements will melt with intense heat! But according to His promise we are* *looking for new heavens and a new earth, in which righteousness dwells (II Peter 3:7-13).*

There is a physical dimension and a spiritual dimension. The earth, the sky, the atmosphere, the moon, the sun, the solar system, galaxies, plants, animals, insects, sea creatures, living humans; all of these things are in the physical dimension. What's in the spiritual dimension? The heavens/heavenlies are there. The throne room of God is there, the part of heaven where the angels exist is there, and there is a place where the righteous dead reside. Hell is there. There is a special hell where God has imprisoned certain demons; there is also a hell where unrighteous humans are imprisoned, until the final day of judgment.

So the spiritual dimension has good and bad within it: heaven with all its levels, and hell with its levels. In our spirits we can be there, although God does limit our access to the levels of hell, and to that part of heaven that the righteous dead reside in. Satan and his demons are also limited in access. The notion that Satan is in hell, ruling over all his little demons is not supported by Scripture. God is the one who created hell, for some demons and unrighteous humans, and He is the master of it. There is no part of the spiritual dimension that is ruled by Satan.

We can sense, understand and walk in the spiritual dimension. I like to think of it this way: it's a really big place: the good parts (heavenlies, including the throne room of God) that we have access to, the really bad parts (hell) that we do not have access to, and a whole lot of space in between (neutral?) that we have access to, along with good angels and bad demons. The good thing is that since God is in us, and his angels work with us, we can confidently walk everywhere God wants us to be in the spiritual dimension.

The present heavens and earth will be destroyed by fire.

The Scriptures quoted at the beginning of this chapter talk about the future, when there will be new heavens and a new earth. It is exciting to think about the wonderful future described. The present heavens and earth (that's the spiritual dimension and the physical dimension) will be destroyed by fire. The heavens will pass away with a roar as the very elements are destroyed by intense heat. The earth will also be burned up. There is definitely an element of judgment in this, as the earth "and all its works" are burned up. Because of sin, committed by ungodly men (and by ungodly angels), both the heavens and the earth are reserved for judgment.

In the midst of all this description, it points out clearly that God is in no hurry to carry out this destruction. He is indifferent to time (a day is as a thousand years, and vice-versa). But He is intensely interested in and devoted to the salvation of mankind (not willing that any should perish, but that all would come to repentance). But...the day of judgment will eventually come.

God promises that the new heavens and new earth (the spiritual dimension and the physical dimension) will be wonderful. There will be no sin or sinners; there will be no Satan or demons; only God's people and His angels. In the new heavens and new earth righteousness will dwell. I don't know how it will work, but the physical world will be so different: no more corruption, and we will freely go back and forth between the two dimensions. We will be in our new spiritual bodies, and I don't know what that will be like, because we won't just be a spirit; we will have "spiritual containers." There will be no corruption. Everything you see described in Revelation chapters 21 and 22 is beautiful, spectacular, everlasting...and righteous!

We love the life God has given us. This present created physical world has so much beauty, and there is so much that we enjoy. I have had the privilege of seeing so many beautiful places as we have traveled in our motor home over the last few years. And the abundant life that we have in the Lord Jesus Christ is wonderful. And if you are like me, food is awesome! Every day as I awaken and breathe in, I am so thankful that I live and move and have my being in the Lord. Over the last few years I have grown to appreciate the spiritual dimension also. I love the tender, instantaneous communication I have with the Holy Spirit within me. In His presence the spiritual dimension is deep and meaningful. As some people have said: "I could die a happy man!" But all of that pales in comparison to the new heavens and new earth. John did his best to describe it in the end of Revelation, but I think that still barely scratches the surface. What we do know is that it will be full of righteousness: new heavens and a new earth in which righteousness dwells.

"O Lord, thank You for this beautiful world, and thank You for the awesome future new heavens and new earth!"

IN CLOSING

What I want for you, and what God wants for all of us is that we sense, understand and walk in the spiritual dimension, just like he intended that we do. He has created us with a physical body, soul and spirit, so that we could function in the physical world through our physical bodies, and in the spiritual world through our spirits. Our physical body is simply our container. Right now it takes a physical form; when it wears out we will move to our next container, a spiritual one. Our soul is the real "us," our mind, our emotions and our will. Our spirit is that part of us that lives and moves in the spiritual. Just as we sense the physical dimension with our five physical senses, so we are to sense the spiritual dimension with our spirit eyes, ears and feelings. God wants us to successfully function in the physical dimension and have abundant life. In the same way He wants us to successfully function in the spiritual dimension and have victorious life. We must not shy away from the spiritual dimension just because we are so comfortable in our physical bodies. Let's wrap our minds around God's spiritual protocol, and let's do what we need to do to become comfortable in our spirits and in the spiritual dimension. First and foremost, let's practice being aware of the spiritual dimension. Secondly, tune our spiritual vision, hearing and feeling to sense whatever is happening in the spiritual dimension. Then let's be the wrestling, fighting warriors that our God intends us to be. Jesus Christ has the highest position and power in the heavens; He shares that power with us. Greater is He that is within us, than Satan who is in the world! We are the forceful people to storm the spiritual dimension with force and win every battle for our Lord Jesus Christ. Ready...set...charge!

ABOUT THE AUTHOR

Reed Tibbetts has served for over twenty-three years as an ordained pastor and teacher, and is currently serving as one of the elders of VLife Church in McKinney, Texas, where he ministers as a prophet and teacher.

An honored and decorated disabled veteran of the Vietnam War, Reed is a graduate of Northwest University of the Assemblies of God. Over the many years he has pursued the goal of handling accurately the word of truth, and has developed a reputation as a guardian of apostolic doctrine (the teachings of the apostles).

Through the years Reed has written and printed many teaching notebooks in the churches he has served, but only recently has he turned to the writing and publishing of books for the greater body of Christ.

Reed lives in Princeton, Texas with his wife of forty-six years. They have three adult children and four grandchildren, all of whom are faithfully serving the Lord in their respective local churches.

AUTHOR CONTACT

Reed has written several other books about the successful Christian life. If you would like to contact him, find out more information, purchase books, or request him to speak, please contact:

Allegro Ministries
470 San Remo
Princeton, TX 75407
yahovah3@gmail.com
214 724-7541

Allegro Ministries is a non-profit corporation, formed by Reed and his family, recognized as a 501(c)(3) by the I.R.S. It exists for the purpose of spreading relevant teachings to the church of the Lord Jesus Christ, so that more and more people can live the brisk and lively Christian walk. If you would like to contribute to the ministry, please send your offerings to the above address, and thank you for your giving.